A DAD'S Blessing

Gary Smalley
and John Trent, Ph.D.
with Mark Wheeler

A
JANET
THOMA
BOOK

THOMAS NELSON PUBLISHERS
Nashville

Published in Nashville, Tennessee, by Janet Thoma Books, a division of Thomas Nelson, Inc., and distributed in Canada by Word Communications, Ltd., Richmond, British Columbia, and in the United Kingdom by Word (UK), Ltd., Milton Keynes, England.

Unless otherwise indicated, Scripture quotations are from THE NEW KING JAMES VERSION of the Bible. Copyright © 1979, 1980, 1982, Thomas Nelson, Inc., Publishers.

Scripture noted KJV is from the King James Version of the Bible.

Scripture quotations noted NIV are from The Holy Bible: NEW INTERNATIONAL VERSION. Copyright © 1978 by the New York International Bible Society. Used by permission of Zondervan Bible Publishers.

Library of Congress Cataloging-in-Publication Data

Smalley, Gary.
    A dad's blessing / Gary Smalley, John Trent.
       p. cm.
    ISBN 0-8407-7792-2
    1. Fathers—Prayer-books and devotions. I. Trent, John T. II. Title.
BV4846.S62 1994
242'.6421—dc20   93–8913
                           CIP

Printed in the United States of America

2 3 4 5 — 96 95

Introduction

Bless me,—me also, O my father!" (Gen. 27:34) was Esau's bitter cry after he was cheated out of receiving his father's blessing by his younger brother, Jacob. Today, many men and women echo Esau's cry sensing the loss or absence of their parents' blessing.

We, Gary and John, also felt the lack of unconditional love and acceptance from our fathers. It was this lack that prompted the writing of our best-selling book *The Blessing*. Now, over nine years later, we are still amazed by the impact the concept of the blessing has on people's lives.

As fathers, we know how important it is to be deliberate in showing love and acceptance to our children. Time constraints and job pressures all too often get in the way of providing them with life-long acceptance and compassion. It is for you, as a father, that we have developed this book. In its pages you will find the original components of the blessing—Meaningful Touch, Spoken Words, Expressing High Value, Picturing a Special Future, and An Active Commitment—related to you in the lives and experiences of others. We have also included a special look at 1 Corinthians 16:13–14 (NIV) as a model for fathering, "Be on your guard; stand firm in the faith; be men of courage; be strong. Do everything in love."

Do not let this opportunity pass you by. Take the next year to make your children a priority and give them your blessing every day of their lives.

Gary Smalley   John Trent

About the Authors

Gary Smalley, president of Today's Family, is a doctoral candidate in marriage and family counseling and has a master's degree from Bethel Seminary in St. Paul, Minnesota. His previous best-selling books include *If Only He Knew, For Better or for Best, Joy That Lasts, The Key to Your Child's Heart,* and *The Blessing.* Gary is the father of three children and lives with his wife, Norma, in Branson, Missouri.

John Trent, president of his own ministry, Encouraging Words, has a Ph.D. in marriage and family counseling and holds a master's degree from Dallas Theological Seminary. In addition to the "Love Is a Decision" seminars he conducts with Gary Smalley, John Trent holds "Blessing" seminars across the country. He wrote with Gary the best-selling books *The Blessing, The Gift of the Blessing, The Gift of Honor, The Language of Love, Love Is a Decision,* and *The Two Sides of Love.* He lives in Phoenix with his wife, Cynthia, and daughters, Kari Lorraine and Laura Catherine.

JANUARY

Promises You Make to Yourself

> *. . . let us run with endurance the race that is set*
> *before us, looking unto Jesus, the author and*
> *finisher of our faith, . . .*   —HEB. 12:1–2

The story is often told of the tortoise and the hare. The hare was a sprint man, county champion in the 100-yard dash. He set a warren record in that event at the Berry Patch Invitational. The tortoise, however, was a marathon man. While he never won any races, he always finished strong and even shaved a few seconds off his time with each race he entered.

As the story goes, they challenged each other to a race in each one's specialty. The tortoise failed miserably in the 100-yard dash. He was just coming out of the starting blocks when the hare crossed the finish line. By the time he finished, the hare had already eaten the victory wreath. But the marathon was another story. Once again, the hare was off to a blazing start. But after sprinting 500 yards, he developed cramps in his side and legs and had to withdraw from the race. Meanwhile, the tortoise, slow but sure, finished the race in grand style.

We are involved in a marathon—life. The secret is not how well we start, but how well we finish. As we raise and nurture our children, we need to provide them with a Godly example of persistence and faithfulness.

Father, may you grant me the grace to finish well.

. . . forgetting those things which are behind and
reaching forward to those things which are ahead,
I press toward the goal for the prize of the upward
call of God in Christ Jesus. —PHIL. 3:13–14

Progress, as defined by Webster, means movement forward. Progress, as defined by life, is three steps forward, two steps back; three steps forward, two steps back. Progress, by either definition, is accomplished by persevering through problems. Perseverance, according to Webster, means persistence; steadfast pursuit of an undertaking or aim. The quality of perseverance is an essential quality for all who want to grow in the Christian life.

The nature of the Christian life is that as we grow toward Christ-likeness, we will invariably stumble and fall. There will be times when we say things we shouldn't; when we have thoughts and feelings we're ashamed to admit; when we react defensively to a simple suggestion. But rather than cry and give up, we pick ourselves up, confess our sins, and keep heading toward the goal of conformity with Christ. A wise person once said that success in the Christian life is simply getting up one more time than you fall.

Lord, help me to get up, forget the past, and pursue the prize.

So that He may establish your hearts blameless in holiness before our God and Father at the coming of our Lord Jesus Christ with all His saints.
—1 THESS. 3:13

A few weeks ago, Roger's family was shopping for groceries. As they rounded a corner, he looked down at his two-year-old daughter who was riding in the basket. She was holding the carton of eggs. The carton was open and revealed that several of the eggs were broken and others were cracked. His first thought was, "Let's just put the carton back and get another. No one will notice."

Sometimes the same temptation occurs when one stays overnight in a motel. Occasionally, the thought comes to mind, "Why not watch one of those late night cable channels? Who's going to know?"

In both of these instances, and in countless others, it is helpful to ask yourself the question, "Who am I when no one's looking? Am I consistent, or do I act differently? Am I the same person Monday through Saturday that I am on Sunday? Will I be blameless and holy when I meet the Lord?"

Father, help me to ooze integrity from the core to the crust. Grant me the grace to be an integrity-driven person.

For as he thinks in his heart, so is he.
—PROV: 23:7

Believe it or not, the IRS received a letter that read, "Dear Sirs: For the last year my conscience has bothered me because I lied on last year's income tax return by not reporting my true income. Enclosed is a check for $150. If my conscience continues to bother me, I'll send in the rest."

In Psalm 15, David states that the person who is welcome in God's presence is one who *"speaks the truth in his heart (v. 2)"*. He doesn't just speak it outwardly. His whole character is truthful. Proverbs 23:7 tells us that as a man *"thinks in his heart, so is he."* What he says inwardly is a characteristic of his entire lifestyle. Instead of merely speaking truth, the righteous person lives truth.

Integrity goes beyond honesty. Integrity is conforming reality to our words, keeping promises, and fulfilling expectations.

Lord, help my life match my words. Help me to live truthfully.

LORD, who may abide in Your tabernacle? Who may dwell in Your holy hill? He who walks uprightly, and works righteousness, and speaks the truth in his heart.
—PS. 15:1–2

Adam Clarke was an assistant in a dry goods store, selling silks and satins to a cultured clientele. One day, his employer suggested to him that he try stretching the silk as he measured it out; this would increase sales and profits, and also increase Adam's value to the company. Young Clarke straightened up from his work, faced his boss courageously, and said, "Sir, your silk may stretch, but my conscience won't."

Unfortunately, some of us are not so honest. The book *The Day America Told the Truth*[1] reported the following: 91 percent of those surveyed admitted to lying about something on a regular basis; 50 percent procrastinate, in effect doing nothing, one full day out of every five; and 74 percent steal from those who will not miss it. Examples of such stealing include taking office supplies from work, long lunches, extravagant meals, accepting gifts from customers, ignoring copyright laws, claiming improper deductions, etc. But the man of integrity avoids all such temptations. He is ethically righteous.

Lord, help me to act in an ethical, honorable manner.

In whose eyes a vile person is despised, but he honors those who fear the LORD . . . —PS. 15:4

Paul attended a conference held on a university campus. Right next door to where the conference was being held, an NBA team was trying out people for the NBA draft. The team's brain trust and coaching staff were there watching as college stars would go one-on-one with current members of the team, including some who were NBA All-Stars. He said it was fun to watch. In fact, so many people from the conference crowded around the open door that they were told to stop doing it or they would lose all access to the building.

The person of integrity is not caught up in a celebrity mentality. He places value on people who put God first and who live for him.

_____

Father, help me view life and people through your eyes.

. . . who keeps his oath even when it hurts.
—PS. 15:4b (NIV)

A general contractor in Texas once signed a contract to build a water park for a large city. After signing the contract, however, he discovered that he had left something substantial out of his estimate. Instead of making a profit, he stood to lose $200,000! Yet, because he was a man of integrity, he resolved to fulfill the contract. Fortunately for him, the city later canceled it.

A person of integrity keeps his promises even if it will cost him something. He *"keeps his oath even when it hurts"* (Ps. 15:4 NIV). This means that once he makes a promise he keeps his word, even if circumstances change so that he is at a disadvantage.

Father, help me to keep my promises even if the price is high.

If you lend money to any of My people who are poor among you, you shall not be like a moneylender to him; you shall not charge him interest.

—EX. 22:25

On his way to school, a young man found two canvas sacks lying in the street. When he looked inside he was amazed to see that the sacks were full of money— $415,000, in fact! When he returned the money to the Princeton Armored Service, he received a reward of $1,000. However, the youth was unhappy because he had expected a larger reward. "I don't understand it," he complained. "If I had to do it all over again, I'd probably keep the money."

A person of integrity is one who *lends his money without usury* (Ps. 15:5 NIV). In that culture, when one's fellow Israelite borrowed money, it meant that he was absolutely destitute. According to God's law, his fellow countrymen were not to take advantage of him by charging interest that he would never be able to repay.

In the same way, a true worshiper of God is not going to take advantage of another's misfortune by putting out his money or time or possessions at interest. Rather than take advantage of someone when they're down, he'll be a good Samaritan.

Father, help me to meet the needs of others rather than take advantage of them when they are hurting.

PROMISES TO YOURSELF

I will praise You with my whole heart; before the gods I will sing praises to You. I will worship toward Your holy temple, and praise Your name for Your lovingkindness and Your truth; for You have magnified Your word above all Your name.

—PS. 138:1–2

When it's springtime and the air is crisp and clean, I feel thankful. But when it's ninety-five degrees and smoggy, and I'm stuck in rush-hour traffic and the car overheats, then I have to choose to be thankful. True thanksgiving involves making the choice in spite of unpleasant circumstances. In Psalm 138:7 David wrote, "Though I walk in the midst of trouble, thou wilt revive me: thou shalt stretch forth thine hand against the wrath of mine enemies, and thy right hand shall save me." You have to admit that's a pretty stressful situation. And yet he said in verses 1 and 2, "I will praise . . . I will worship . . ." David made the choice to be thankful in the midst of his troubles.

In order to give thanks in the midst of bad situations, we have to make two suppositions: one, in spite of everything, God is still sovereign and he is in control; and two, God does not make mistakes. We can be confident of his love and care.

Lord, help me to choose to say, "Thank you!"

*Brethren, I do not count myself to have
apprehended; but one thing I do, forgetting those
things which are behind and reaching forward to
those things which are ahead, I press toward the
goal for the prize of the upward call of God in
Christ Jesus.*
                                        —PHIL. 3:13–14

Dale positioned himself on the ledge of the rocky
crag. Facing the rocks, he hung on tightly to a gnarled
root with his left hand. He strained with his right hand
to reach the next handhold. As hard as he strained,
and even though it was only inches away, he could not
reach it. He was stuck.

As he contemplated his dilemma, he realized he was
going to have to let go of the security of the root in
order to reach the handhold that would get him off the
ledge. But fear paralyzed his decision.

Many times we are like Dale. In order to move into
the future, and become the person God wants us to be,
we have to let go of the past in order to press onward
to reach the goals that God has for us.

*Father, help me to trust you enough to give up the security of the
past in order to reach out for your desires for my future.*

But he said to them, "Do not be alarmed. You seek Jesus of Nazareth, who was crucified. He is risen! He is not here. See the place where they laid Him. But go and tell His disciples—and Peter—that He is going before you into Galilee; there you will see Him, as He said to you."
—MARK 16:6–7

The pages of history are filled with failures, including some that are rather amusing. How about the California sunbather who decided to acquire the perfect tan? He heard you could get better tanning rays above the urban smog so he attached forty-two helium balloons to his deck chair, which he had tethered to the earth with a long rope. Unfortunately, the rope broke and he rose to 15,000 feet where a passing airline pilot reported him as a UFO!

Most of us operate from the unspoken belief that failure is fatal. This philosophy hinders us from taking risks and disqualifies us from ever trying again. When we fail we may consider ourselves losers. When this happens, we need a large dose of hope and forgiveness to restore us. We need someone to tell us that God can transform a horrible failure into a hopeful future. (See John 21:15–19 for how Jesus restored Peter following the resurrection.) We need to be reminded that we serve the God of the second chance.

Father, remind me that while failure is painful, it is seldom fatal.

*And Achan answered Joshua and said, "Indeed I
have sinned against the LORD God of Israel . . ."*
—JOSH. 7:20

There are many ways to have a flat tire on a bicycle:
adding too much air can cause a tire to explode because of the force of the air pressure; or accidentally
riding over a nail will suddenly flatten it. More often,
however, is the flat you discover because the air slowly
leaked out over time. Maybe it happened because of
a pin-sized hole or simply a weakened area in the tire
wall.

Failure like Achan's is seldom a blowout. It is usually
a slow leak over a period of time. A compromise in
values here, a little "white" lie there, fudging on an
expense report—all weaken the walls of one's character. Then, when temptation comes, we give in. It may
appear that we had a blowout, but the reality is that
the walls were simply too thin to withstand any more
pressure from temptation.

Rather than allow my convictions to be compro-
mised, I must guard my heart.

*Father, make my conduct consistent with my character and my con-
victions.*

> *I will give her her vineyards from there, and the*
> *Valley of Achor as a door of hope; she shall sing*
> *there, as in the days of her youth, as in the day*
> *when she came up from the land of Egypt.*
> —HOS. 2:15

Perhaps you have a mistake or failure that you have tried to bury, but still it remains heavy upon you like a pile of rocks. Maybe you stole something and told some lies to cover it up. Perhaps you had an affair. Maybe it's a drinking problem or an ugly divorce. You confessed it and made restitution, but there's still a pile of rocks that reminds you of your failure.

That sense of failure cripples you emotionally. As a result, you are ready to run up a white flag, or to abandon ship. "There is no point in going further," you tell yourself. "Once a loser, always a loser." At times like this, we desperately need to be reassured that failure is not fatal.

When God restored the Jews to Israel, the Valley of Achor, once a visual reminder of failure and trouble (see Joshua 7), would become a symbol of a fresh start. Isaiah 65:10 explains that the Valley of Achor would become a place of rest. In addition, Hosea explains that it would become a door of hope. A pile of rocks marking the grave of failure would become the cornerstone of a door of new opportunity.

Father, thank you that my failures are forgiven and forgotten. Help me to understand this.

*Not that I speak in regard to need, for I have
learned in whatever state I am, to be content.*
—PHIL. 4:11

Contentment is not standard equipment for every infant born into the human race. Do you know what most children wanted last year for Christmas? "More!" More presents, more candy, more stories from Grandma and Grandpa. More, more, and more! Lest we be too hard on children, the wealthy John D. Rockefeller was once asked, "How much does it take to satisfy a man?" With rare wisdom he answered, "A little bit more than he has."

In Philippians 4:11, Paul says that he learned to be content. This type of learning comes less by instruction and more by experience. Paul learned to be content in the extremes of life. In v. 12, he states, "Everywhere and in all things I have learned both to be full and to be hungry, both to abound and to suffer need." He knew how to do without and he knew how to live the good life.

Contentment is a mystery which the average person does not know or understand. Ask most people and they will not have a clue as to how or where they can find contentment. It is a secret that needs to be discovered.

Lord, help me to learn to be content with what you provide.

Let us draw near with a true heart in full
assurance of faith, having our hearts sprinkled
from an evil conscience and our bodies washed
with pure water.
—HEB. 10:22

As Scott scurried through the airport trying to catch his flight, he was delayed at the metal detector. He impatiently emptied his keys, loose coins, pocket knife, and belt buckle trying to shut off the persistent nuisance of the alarm meant to detect weapons carried by would-be terrorists.

Interestingly enough, one palace of Changan, the ancient capital of what is now Thailand, had a similar device. The gates of the capital were made of lodestone (a natural magnet). When a would-be assassin would try to come through the gate with a concealed dagger, the lodestone would pull at the hidden weapon like an invisible hand. Startled, the individual would involuntarily reach for the weapon. Watchful guards would then grab and disarm the intruder.

In much the same way, a healthy conscience tugs at the concealed sins in our lives as though it were God's hidden hand. As we attempt to enter God's presence, it sounds off the warning alarm of guilt which prods us to empty our wrong deeds and attitudes upon the table. When the buzzers have gone off, it allows us to freely proceed and to stand boldly before the Father.

Lord, when the buzzer sounds, help me to remove any attitude or action that sets off the alarm.

PROMISES TO YOURSELF

Now the word of the LORD came to Jonah the second time . . .
—JONAH 3:1

On New Year's Day, 1929, Georgia Tech played UCLA in the Rose Bowl. In that game, a man named Roy Riggles of UCLA recovered a fumble, became confused, and started running sixty-five yards in the wrong direction. One of his teammates, Benny Lom, outdistanced him and tackled him just before he scored for the opposing team. Eventually, UCLA attempted to punt, Tech blocked the kick and scored a safety—which was the ultimate margin of victory.

At halftime, Riggles sat down in a corner and sobbed. Coach Nibbs Price walked over to Riggles and said, "Roy, get up and go on back. The game is only half over." And Riggles went back and played as he never had before.

Like Roy Riggles, we pick up the ball and run in the wrong direction. We stumble, fall, and make mistakes. We sit dejectedly and never want to try again. And God comes to us, and through his word and his Son says, "Get up, the game's only half over." The gospel of the grace of God is the gospel of the second chance and the third chance and the hundredth chance. It is the gospel of Jonah, for Peter, for you and me.

Father, when I fall, remind me that the game is only half over.

PROMISES TO YOURSELF

*I will extol You, my God, O King; and I will bless
Your name forever and ever. Every day I will bless
You, and I will praise Your name forever and ever.*
—PS. 145:1–2

Ellen was out shopping one day when she developed
some car problems. Ever the gracious husband, Phil
rescued her, sent her home, and stayed with the car
while he waited for the tow truck. Seven and a half
hours, one newspaper, two magazines, and four diet
sodas later, he called the company for the sixth time.
Unfortunately they had gotten the address wrong and
had sent the truck to the wrong location. When it
wasn't there, they went home and forgot about him.

Needless to say, Phil had a very difficult time praising God in that situation. He did not like what God was
doing, and it was extremely hard to be thankful. Yet,
according to Scripture, he realized that he had the responsibility to praise God.

Throughout Psalms, David seldom says, "I feel
thankful." But he quite often says, "I will give thanks."
In order to praise God every day, regardless of the situation, we have to make the conscious choice to bless
him. We have to choose to praise him even when we
may not understand or like what he is doing.

*Father, help me to choose to say, "Thank you," today for the situa-
tions and people I encounter.*

*My mouth shall speak the praise of the LORD, and
all flesh shall bless His holy name forever and ever.*
—PS. 145:21

Jamie Scott was a young schoolboy who was trying
out for a part in the school play. His mother, a sensitive
woman, knew that he had set his heart on being in it.
However, she was afraid that he would not be chosen
and that his heart would be broken. On the day the
parts were awarded, she drove to school to pick him
up. Little Jamie rushed up to the car, eyes shining with
pride and excitement. "Guess what, Mom? I've been
chosen to clap and cheer."

As believers, we have been chosen to clap and
cheer and to praise the glory of God. Rather than
grouse and complain our way through life, God wants
us to have a heart of joy and thanksgiving. In fact, we
are commanded to praise God for his attributes and his
actions; to declare who he is and what he has done in
our lives. He wants us to get a head start, since we'll
do it for all eternity.

*Lord, help me to play the role that you have chosen for me and cause
me to have a heart that praises you.*

Therefore we do not lose heart. Even though our outward man is perishing, yet the inward man is being renewed day by day. —2 COR. 4:16

When Burt was in college, he went through a two-year period where he had boils on his body. Some were more visible and quite embarrassing as they drained. Others affected his activities.

Every few weeks found him in the doctors' office having one lanced and drained. He had blood tests to determine if there was a treatable cause and to discover a cure. The doctors were puzzled when they could not find one. Then as mysteriously as the boils appeared, they mysteriously disappeared.

During this time, he learned the truth of 2 Corinthians 4:16. His body was literally wasting away. The best thing Burt could do was to renew and strengthen his walk with God. He caught a momentary glimpse of the truth that this body is temporary and one day he would receive a body that never suffers from sickness.

Father, renew and refashion my attitudes so that they reflect what you want them to.

"Woe to you, scribes and Pharisees, hypocrites! For you are like whitewashed tombs which indeed appear beautiful outwardly, but inside are full of dead men's bones and all uncleanness. Even so you also outwardly appear righteous to men, but inside you are full of hypocrisy and lawlessness . . ."

—MATT. 23:27–28

Garbage trucks can appear to be attractive on the outside: freshly painted, shiny metal vehicles with smoothly operating hydraulics. You might even consider parking such a fine looking machine in your driveway—until you see it drive to the landfill, open up the rear panel, and dump out its contents. Then you realize it carries a revolting, stinking mass of garbage.

Jesus condemned the Pharisees because they were more concerned with polishing an illusion than with throwing out the garbage. Rather than clean out the rotten, moldy garbage, they bought air freshener and car wax. They spent hours buffing the shine so that they could see their reflection, but they couldn't understand why the flies wouldn't go away.

Where is your attention focused? What is the fragrance of your relationships at home or in the office? Do you need to fumigate some bitterness and resentment that has been growing in the corner of your heart?

Father, clean out my heart and remove anything that offends you.

PROMISES TO YOURSELF

*Bretheren, I do not count myself to have
apprehended; but one thing I do, forgetting those
things which are behind and reaching forward to
those things which are ahead, I press toward the
goal for the prize of the upward call of God in
Christ Jesus.*
                                    —PHIL. 3:13–14

We should approach important goals like an Olympic sprinter in the 100-meter dash. His life has been focused on winning this event. He takes off his warmups, sets himself in the blocks, and gets ready for the starting gun. As he lifts his head, he looks down the lane, focused on the finishing tape. As the gun sounds, he bolts out of the blocks, kicks in the afterburners, and strains with every fiber of his being for the finish.

In order to accomplish his objectives, Paul employs the principle of planned neglect. In Philippians 3:3–11, he takes a hard look at all his assets and says he is *willing to lay them all aside in order to know God better.* In 3:13, he forgets the past. He chooses to no longer be influenced or affected by the past. He plans to neglect anything that hinders him from focusing on his goal.

As men, we need to establish priorities in our lives that will allow us to accomplish what God has called us to do and to be. Then, we must neglect anything that hinders us from accomplishing them. We must pursue and press on toward the goal of godliness.

Father, help me to strain and stretch toward godliness.

PROMISES TO YOURSELF

> *For I say, through the grace given to me, to
> everyone who is among you, not to think of himself
> more highly than he ought to think, but to think
> soberly, as God has dealt to each one a measure of
> faith.*
> —ROM. 12:3

I understand you are an expert in astrophysics. Peter said that if I had any questions I should come to you," explained Sam to Adam.

Adam could reply to this complimentary statement in several ways. He could modestly say, "Well, he has more confidence in me than I have in me. He's just saying that to be nice." Or he could arrogantly state, "He's right, you know. There's not a thing about that subject that I don't know. But you couldn't possibly understand any of it. It's far too complex for your little mind." Or he might reply with gracious self-esteem.

When it comes to receiving compliments, we usually err to one extreme or the other, either to pride or to false humility. Instead, Scripture encourages us to have an accurate view of ourselves. Rather than be intoxicated with our own success, or completely abstain from tasting our achievements, we are to think soberly and have a balanced self-image.

Father, help me to maintain an accurate and honest view of myself in regard to strengths, weaknesses, and achievements. Help me to see myself as you see me.

My brethren, count it all joy when you fall into various trials, knowing that the testing of your faith produces patience. But let patience have its perfect work, that you may be perfect and complete, lacking nothing.
—JAMES 1:2–4

Have you heard about the microwave fireplace? You can enjoy a complete, romantic evening in front of the fireplace in just three minutes. While that may not be realistic, we certainly have come to rely on microwave ovens. You can fix an entire meal in less time than it takes to open the box (or so they say).

When it comes to spiritual growth, God seldom uses a microwave oven. More often than not, he uses a slow cooker which softens and tenderizes even the toughest and most callused heart. He turns up the heat of trials, sets us on the back burner of life, and allows us to simmer until we are done. Like a pot roast with onions and potatoes thrown in, we lack nothing when the process is complete.

Have you ever taken the lid off a crock pot partway through cooking? While it allows you to smell the aroma, it lengthens the cooking time and robs the meal of some of the flavor. Waiting the full eight to ten hours allows you to fully savor the taste of the meal inside. In the same way, God also rewards those who persevere in the midst of trials. A crown is waiting for those who stand the test.

Father, help me to endure and persevere.

*Who is wise and understanding among you? Let
him show by good conduct that his works are done
in the meekness of wisdom.* —JAMES 3:13

Some of the smartest people are also the dumbest.
One individual had two master's degrees and a doctoral degree, but had no common sense at all. He could
converse on microbiology, but would forget to wear a
coat in the rain.

A key principle for living, as James points out, is that
wisdom is shown by deeds, not degrees. Like faith, it
is demonstrated in the crucible of life. As faith is demonstrated by works, so wisdom is revealed in a
changed life.

The biblical idea of wisdom is not merely intellectual
understanding and perception—it is skill for living. It
is not enough to merely know right—wisdom is doing
what is right. A truly wise person is one who has moral
insight and skill in the practical issues of life. Knowledge is not enough—you must be able to use it.

---

*Father, grant me the ability to put into practice what I know to be
right.*

> *Therefore be patient, brethren, until the coming of the Lord. See how the farmer waits for the precious fruit of the earth, waiting patiently for it until it receives the early and latter rain.* —JAMES 5:7

Tim laced up his running shoes with strong, deliberate pulls on the laces. He yanked so hard that he broke both of them. He was still fuming from the day's events.

He had left the board meeting seething because of some of the comments that had been made. And because of the way he felt, he had intentionally avoided contact with anyone else. He was afraid he would say something he would later regret. So he hurried home, grabbed his jogging clothes, and went to the track at the high school.

As he ran, he mumbled his anger and resentment aloud. He allowed his pent-up frustration to pour through his body into the surface below. As the track cushioned the blows to his feet, so his anger was calmed. By the third mile, he was able to pray for the board members.

The word *patience* in the Bible is a compound word that literally means "long-temper." It is the idea of setting the timer of one's temper for a long run. It is the self-restraint of hasty retaliation.

Lord, help me to be more patient in dealing with people, especially my wife and children.

PROMISES TO YOURSELF

You also be patient. Establish your hearts, for the coming of the Lord is at hand. —JAMES 5:8

John developed a reputation as being a hard worker. When the other employees would stretch their coffee break to twenty or thirty minutes, John was already back at his desk, working on his assignment. Whenever he ran out of work, he would either ask for more or start cleaning around his desk. He knew that the boss had the habit of popping in unexpectedly, and if he did that today, he wanted to be hard at work.

James explains that the soon return of Jesus Christ should motivate us to get and stay ready. He encourages us to stand firm or, literally, to strengthen our hearts. That phrase became an idiom for steadfastness or being ready. The mature believer is strong in the inner man and able to withstand difficulties and trials and is unmoved by trouble because he wants to be ready should Jesus return at any moment. Rather than be caught off guard, he remains alert.

Lord, help me to be on the lookout for your return and help me not to be ashamed and unprepared when that happens.

> *Therefore be patient, brethren, until the coming of*
> *the Lord. See how the farmer waits for the precious*
> *fruit of the earth, waiting patiently for it until it*
> *receives the early and latter rain.* —JAMES 5:7

Last spring, Larry's wife and children planted a garden in the backyard. When the radishes started coming up, they were excited because they were going to eat fresh vegetables that they grew themselves! After a few days, they discovered that the radishes weren't growing any bigger and the leaves were turning brown. Puzzled, they began calling various nurseries to figure what they were doing wrong.

One afternoon, Larry's wife happened to see their four-year-old daughter talking in the garden. Curious, she eavesdropped to discover what was going on. The girl was talking to a radish in her hand. It turned out she had been pulling the radishes out each day to see how much they had grown overnight! She expected them to get bigger and talked to them when they didn't grow.

How often do we expect immediate or overnight growth in others?

Father, help me to wait patiently for you to work in my life and in the lives of others.

He who answers a matter before he hears it, it is folly and shame to him.
—PROV. 18:13

Dear," said Myrna, "did you see this article in the . . . ?"

"Are you reading that stupid paper again?" asked George.

"It talks about the communication pattern of husbands and wives and how . . ." started his wife.

George interrupted, "You know you can't believe everything you read."

". . . husbands interrupt their wives most of the time."

Does this pattern sound familiar in your household? For most husbands, if we are not interrupting verbally, we're probably doing it mentally: rehearsing a response before we even know the question. And more often than not, we're embarrassed because we weren't paying attention to what was actually said and consequently our answer or retort is way off the mark.

Father, help me to have ears that hear.

Come now, you who say, "Today or tomorrow we will go to such and such a city, spend a year there, buy and sell, and make a profit"; whereas you do not know what will happen tomorrow. For what is your life? It is even a vapor that appears for a little time and then vanishes away. Instead you ought to say, "If the Lord wills, we shall live and do this or that."

—JAMES 4:13–15

Evan Welsh, the former chaplain of Wheaton College, had the habit of filling his day with appointments and personal contacts with students, faculty, alumni, and members of the community. At the top of each page of his appointment schedule was printed the initials: D. V. When asked what it meant, he explained that they stood for the Latin phrase *Deo Volente,* "God willing." Even though he had filled his schedule as he thought best, he recognized that all of it or none of it would be accomplished, but only if the Lord was willing.

On the day of his death, he had a full schedule of appointments, but written above was D. V. On that day, God was not willing for him to fulfill his commitment. Instead, he had a more important appointment for him to keep, an audience with the King of the universe.

Lord, help me to plan and schedule my life Deo Volente.

*I went by the field of the slothful . . . all overgrown
with thorns; its surface was covered with nettles;*
—PROV. 24:30–31

If it wasn't for the moss and dandelions, I wouldn't
have a lawn at all!" Steve said to himself. "They keep
the yard green."

They had moved into a house in November. In the
spring, when everything started turning green and
growing again, the moss and weeds took over the
lawn. You could barely see the grass. It was evident
that the previous tenants did not keep up the lawn.

For several weeks, he and his wife spent their free
time pulling weeds and trying to get the yard in shape.
As he dug up dandelions, he reflected on his life.
"What weeds have grown up in my life? As a result of
laziness, neglect, or lack of interest, what areas in my
life have withered or been choked by weeds?"

As he knelt in the weeds, he asked God to replant
and renew his devotion, and to restore the greenness,
once again.

―――――――――

Father, renew my commitment to personal growth.

"I have made a covenant with my eyes; Why then should I look upon a young woman?"

—JOB 31:1

As the national sales manager for his securities firm, Jeremy was on the road at least three days out of every five. After two years of countless hotel rooms, he found the boredom setting in. Retiring to his hotel room at night, he began channel surfing with the television, searching for something to catch his interest. Like a moth to a flame, he became increasingly curious about the X-rated cable channels.

Not wanting to give in, he asked the men in his Saturday morning Bible study to hold him accountable to three things. When he arrived at the hotel, he would ask the desk clerk to disconnect his television. The second was that he would maintain a list of and be accountable about the books and magazines that he bought and was currently reading. Finally, whenever he felt tempted morally, he asked permission to call one of the other men, regardless of where he was or the time of day.

Father, help me to willingly make myself accountable to others.

FEBRUARY

Promises You Make
to Your Family

"Until now you have asked nothing in My name. Ask, and you will receive, that your joy may be full."

—JOHN 16:24

On a sunny spring day, Dick and his family decided to venture outdoors and reclaim their garden and lawn from the winter weeds. Mapping out a strategy, they each attacked a stronghold of dandelions and pulled with reckless abandon. Moving through the yard, his daughter encountered a rock in her path. Even in her limited understanding of nature, she knew that it must be moved so that a flower could be planted in its place. Being the industrious young woman that she was, she tried lifting it, but it wouldn't bulge. She tried pushing it and pulling it, but to no avail. She tried wrapping her arms around it, but she couldn't move it.

After watching her ordeal with great interest, Dick ventured over and asked if she had tried everything to move the rock. She replied that she had. He said, "No, you haven't tried everything. You haven't asked me to help you." Realizing her mistake, she accepted his offer, and together they moved the stone.

Father, help me to learn to ask for your help.

*A disciple is not above his teacher, but everyone
who is perfectly trained will be like his teacher.*
—LUKE 6:40

After reading bedtime stories, do you lie down in bed
with your kids? As Sam talked with his daughter about
her day, he propped himself up on his elbow. She did
the same with her elbow. He scrunched up the pillow
and put his head down. She did the same thing with
her pillow. He crossed his leg and so did she. He stuck
out his tongue and winked at her. She did also. No matter what he did, she mimicked him and provided a mirror image of his actions.

As father, we are a model to our children. Much
more than merely mimicking our words, tone or mannerisms, they also pick up our attitudes and values. We
must keep in mind the words of Jesus in Luke 6:40 that
a student's progress is limited by the teaching he receives.

Father, help me to model a consistent message.

Husbands, love your wives, just as Christ also loved the church and gave Himself for it.

—EPH. 5:25

Most men buy flowers for their wives. This usually occurs on those rare occasions when the floral industry mounts a massive campaign that breaks through their resistance and piles up enormous guilt so that they give in and buy a single rose, or maybe some carnations.

The statement has often been made that the best thing you can do for your children is to love their mother. In other words, we need to be more free to let our children see that we love her. We need to do little loving things for her: opening her car door, placing her chair at the table, sending her love letters when we're away from home, or giving her little gifts on special occasions. As we walk in the park or the mall, we need to hold her hand. We should praise her in the presence of our children.

The best way to give our children security and stability in life is to demonstrate that we, their parents, love each other.

_____

Lord, help me to be creative and consistent in showing love to my wife.

And these words which I command you today shall be in your heart; you shall teach them diligently to your children, and shall talk of them when you sit in your house, when you walk by the way, when you lie down, and when you rise up.

—DEUT. 6:6–7

At times, our children have crawled into our laps to talk with us. But far too many times, we have been too engrossed in watching TV, reading the paper or a book, or talking to someone to pay attention and listen to them.

If we want our children to listen to us when they are older, we need to listen and understand what they are saying when they are small. We need to hear their hurts and complaints, their joys and excitement. We need to work hard at refraining from words of impatience at the interruption.

It is estimated that the average child asks 500,000 questions by age fifteen. We need to pay better attention to their questions and look upon it as an opportunity to share our values and convictions as well as our knowledge.

Father, help me to be sensitive and to learn to listen.

Behold, children are a heritage from the LORD.
—PS. 127:3

Her cheeks glowed in the soft flicker of candlelight. Her eyes, brimming with excitement, twinkled with merriment. She inhaled a big breath, and then with great force, she blew out her birthday candles. *"Yeah!"* they all cheered and applauded. *"Happy birthday to you . . ."* the family sang with great enthusiasm and love.

When it comes to birthdays, we should work over-time to make our children feel that their day is special. By working with them to create a birthday placemat, taking the other children shopping for their sibling, or fixing their favorite dinner, we grant them honor and distinction. This is their unique day. We should make certain that the person, rather than the gift, is central. Thus, they will feel a heightened sense of worth, acceptance, value, love, and belonging.

Father, help my children sense they belong and are of high value to me.

*Take heed that you do not despise one of these little
ones, for I say to you that in heaven their angels
always see the face of My Father who is in heaven.*
—MATT. 18:10

The average morning in most homes is a rushed affair
where breakfast is eaten in shifts and consists of a
quick bowl of cereal and some juice. On one holiday
morning, Tim decided to actually fix breakfast so the
family could eat together. As he was preparing some
blueberry muffins, his six-year-old son asked if he
could help. Tim's first thought was to say, "No, you're
too little. You'll just get in the way. You'll slow down
the process and I'm almost done anyway."

Fortunately, what he said was, "Yes, but wash your
hands first. Son, measure out two cups of flour. Good
job, now measure three-fourths-cup of sugar. You did
such a nice job of measuring and pouring that. I'll bet
when you grow up you're going to be a great cook."

Nothing encourages a child to love life, to seek ac-
complishment and to gain confidence more than
proper, sincere praise—not flattery or empty, dishon-
est praise, but honest compliments when he does well.

---

*Father, help me to think highly of my children and to praise them
when they do well.*

. . . redeeming the time, because the days are evil.
—EPH. 5:16

A study was conducted with a group of 300 seventh- and eighth-grade boys. They were asked to keep records of how much time their fathers actually spent with them over a two-week period. The results concluded that most saw their father only at the dinner table. A number never saw their father for days at a time. The average time a father and son were *alone together* for an entire week was only seven and a half minutes!

Arthur Gordon tells an interesting experience from his youth. "When I was around thirteen and my brother was ten, Father promised to take us to the circus. But at lunch there was a phone call; some urgent business required his attention downtown. My brother and I braced ourselves for the disappointment. Then we heard him say, 'No, I won't be down. It will have to wait.' When he came back to the table, Mother smiled. 'The circus keeps coming back, you know.' 'I know,' said Father. 'But childhood doesn't.'"

Father, help me to demonstrate love to my children by rearranging my schedule to spend time with them.

A merry heart does good, like medicine, but a
broken spirit dries the bones. —PROV. 17:22

In the movie *Field of Dreams,* Roy Kinsella makes a statement that he never remembered his father being young and energetic. He only saw him later in life when he was beaten down with care. How will your children remember you?

Let's face it, life has become too serious. As our families grow larger, our responsibilities are stacked higher, and we tend to become too serious. As life becomes busier and harder, our outlook dims. It seems like we are always being followed by a black cloud.

Something needs to change. We need to laugh more often. We need to inject a healthy dose of joy into our lives. Why not resolve to make your home a place where laughter rings in the rafters, where joy is on every face? Make a commitment to study the concept of laughter and joy, and to practice them to a greater degree. Ask yourself the question, "How will my children remember me?"

Father, restore to me the joy of life and salvation.

Likewise you husbands, dwell with them with understanding, giving honor to the wife, as to the weaker vessel, and as being heirs together of the grace of life, that your prayers may not be hindered.

—1 PETER 3:7

Some women collect spoons, plates, pictures, or postcards. Terry's mom collected cups and saucers. In fact, they were all over the house. There were the everyday plastic ones in the cupboard (not even boys could break them). There were china ones for special guests. And there were the hand-painted, ceramic ones that were not used but admired in the cabinet with the glass doors. Each one had a different function and beauty, as well as a unique strength and fragility. Before using them, you had to understand something about their nature and purpose.

In the same way, Peter instructs husbands to live with their wives in an understanding way. We need to have a basic working knowledge about women, in general, and about our wife, specifically. If necessary, check out some books from the library or, heaven forbid, ask her to explain and help you understand.

Father, grant me an open and discerning heart that I might understand my wife.

And you, fathers, do not provoke your children to
wrath, but bring them up in the training and
admonition of the Lord.
—EPH. 6:4

Daddy, can I go outside and play with Jimmy?" "No."
"Can I have chocolate milk for dinner?" "No."
"Can I ride my bike outside?" "No."
"Why can't I do anything?" "Because I said so, that's why! I'm the daddy, and don't you forget it!"

It's easy to frustrate our children when we don't have good reasons as to why we grant or deny a request, or when we are inconsistent in our punishment for breaking rules. We need to think through our convictions and be able to explain them. If we don't have a good reason, we need to admit it.

Father, help me to be sensitive to my children's attitude toward how I discipline them.

Train up a child in the way he should go,
And when he is old he will not depart from it.
—PROV. 22:6

John was concerned that all he ever did was nag his son about his room, chores, clothes, and friends. Trying to break out of that pattern, he decided to observe all the good things his son did for one month and to write them down in a notebook. At the end of the month, his plan was to share them with his son.

He was astounded when he discovered the things his son was involved in. He cried with his son as he read what he had written down. He confessed that he had been so critical because he realized that he was trying to make his son a clone of himself rather than allowing him to express his own individuality.

Rather than forcing our children into a cookie cutter shape, Proverbs 22:6 suggests that we train them according to their own unique design. In order to do that, we need to become a student of our children in order to recognize and understand who they are.

Lord, help me to prize the uniqueness of my children rather than force them to be like me.

*Moreover, as for me, far be it from me that I should
sin against the LORD in ceasing to pray for you; but
I will teach you the good and the right way.*
—1 SAM. 12:23

There are times when our prayers degenerate into
"God bless my wife and kids and keep them safe today,
Amen." While this is not necessarily bad (after all, at
least we are praying for them), it's not necessarily
good because it doesn't address their real needs. In order to be more effective in our prayers, we should turn
to someone for advice, namely, our wives. Why not
brainstorm different categories of needs for both herself as well as the kids? Then incorporate them into
your prayer list, praying for a different category each
day.

For your wife: pray for her role as wife and mother,
her spiritual growth, her physical health, her emotional stability, and her time management. For your
children: pray for their spiritual growth, their physical
health and safety, that they grow intellectually and
develop a love for learning, their choice of friends,
and their future. In addition, pray that they would enjoy their siblings and learn to live peacefully with
them, that they would learn respect and honor for
others, and that they would know that they are loved
and cared for.

*Father, cause me to be diligent in bringing my wife and children be-
fore your throne.*

PROMISES TO FAMILY

Therefore let us pursue the things which make for peace and the things by which one may edify another.

—ROM. 14:19

On a bitterly cold night in the far north of Canada, two porcupines found themselves together in a small cave. Realizing that they would freeze by themselves, they inched toward each other, hoping to gain greater warmth from the other. The closer they drew, the more their sharp quills poked the other. They drew apart, nursing their wounds. Feeling cold again, they inched closer—once again pricking each other. Back and forth they went in their deliberate dance. They needed each other, even though they needled each other.

What a picture of marriage! We long for the warmth and comfort that comes from an intimate relationship, yet when our spouse gets under our skin, we pull away because we are uncomfortable. We want the joy of intimacy without the jabs of insensitivity.

Men, a peaceful home requires that we set the pace and model the type of attitude that we want to see. Rather than wait for our wife or children to act in a more calm manner before we lower our voices, peace depends on us.

Father, help me to disarm my weapons of war and to pursue peace.

Blessed are the peacemakers, for they shall be called sons of God.
                                        —MATT. 5:9

Henry Kissinger, James Baker, Cyrus Vance; United Nations Security Council, multinational forces, holiday cease-fire—peacemakers vs. peacekeepers. If history is accurate in its records, peacemakers achieve fame while peacekeepers accrue frustration. Peacemakers desire lasting change while peacekeepers deliver momentary quiet before the resumption of hostility.

Too often, we may be guilty of merely trying to be a peacekeeper at home. "Go to your room." "Tell your sister you're sorry." "You sit on the couch and you sit in the corner, and don't even look at each other." These are all the words of a peacekeeper, trying to enforce and maintain a temporary cease-fire. But when the time-out is over—when the kids return from their room and get up off the couch—hostility resumes and often escalates.

Peacekeepers are ineffective because they treat symptoms rather than cure diseases. God has not called us to keep the peace, but rather to help make peace, both between God and man as well as between brothers and sisters.

God, help to focus on what will bring lasting peace rather than temporary silence.

If you endure chastening, God deals with y
with sons; for what son is there whom a fa
not chasten?

—HEB. 12:7

A man came up to two boys who were fighting in the park. He took one aside and began to spank him for his inappropriate behavior. An observing by-stander came up to the man and asked indignantly why he didn't do anything to the other boy. The man responded that the one he disciplined was his own son and the other was not.

As fathers, we have made a commitment to nurture, guide, teach, and discipline our children. One of the ways we do this is by becoming personally involved in their instruction and correction. Rather than abdicate our role and responsibility to someone else, we need to think through how we want them to turn out. Having their character in mind helps us to plan and discipline them accordingly. It helps us to know when to protect them from harm and when to let them learn from the natural consequences of their actions.

Father, help me to love my children enough to get involved in their lives and help to shape their future.

Now no chastening seems to be joyful for the present, but grievous; nevertheless, afterward it yields the peaceable fruit of righteousness to those who have been trained by it.
—HEB. 12:11

A young child accidentally took sleeping pills from the family's medicine cabinet. Discovering the deed, the parents frantically called the doctor. He calmly instructed the parents to keep the child awake by any means necessary for the next four hours—including the pain of slapping him, if necessary.

The parents dutifully sat with the child for the time period. Talking with him, they would force him to answer questions and maintain a conversation. They tried to play his favorite game with him. When he would begin to doze off, they would call to him, tickle him, shake him, and yes, slap him occasionally. The pain was necessary for the child's survival.

There are times when our kids will think that we're ogres because we ask them to take out the trash, pick up their toys and clothes, and help do the dishes. They focus on the pain of the moment. Our gaze, however, is fixed on shaping them into people who are helpful, considerate, organized, and orderly.

Lord, help me to think long-term in relationship to developing my children's conduct and character.

Do not withhold correction from a child, for if you beat him with a rod, he will not die. You shall beat him with a rod, and deliver his soul from hell.
—PROV. 23:13–14

It was not a pretty sight! The four-year-old was suffering from an acute case of stubbornness—a very severe case in one of such tender years. Refusing to do what her mother asked, she talked back to her and stomped her feet. Tempers escalated to the point where she kicked her sister, yelled at everyone, and finally spanked her mother on the leg.

Trying to remain impartial, Dad realized that her behavior would become dangerous to all involved if it were to continue. Springing into action, he grabbed her by the waist, picked her up, carried her into her room, gave her the worst spanking of her life, and banished her to her room until dinnertime.

Ten minutes later, he went back to her room to talk with her before dinner. She crawled up on his lap and wrapped her arms around his neck. What she said was not "I'm sorry, Dad," or "I won't do it again," but—with a wisdom and perception far beyond her years—"I love you, Daddy!"

Father, help me to love my children enough to be willing to deal with their misbehavior.

*A soft answer turns away wrath, but a harsh word
stirs up anger.*
                                        —PROV. 15:1

Pulling into the driveway, Dan sensed that armed hostilities had broken out. He could hear the screaming out on the sidewalk. But the tone of his daughter's voice told him that she was beyond anger. Her emotional tank was on empty and she had simply lost it. Rather than pour kerosene on a roaring fire, she needed a cool breeze to calm her down.

He found her standing in the bathroom, brushing her teeth for bed. (You know it's a tough day when the kids are sent to bed at 5:30 P.M.!) Rather than shout at her, he stroked the back of her hair, told her to take a deep breath, and calm down. After she was finished, he held her on his lap, coaxing her into bed. Lying down with her, he quietly talked her through the events that preceded his arrival. Within a few minutes, she was calmly telling him about her day and even laughing at an amusing story. Like a dying fire, the flames went out and the embers cooled down.

---

*Lord, help me to provide a cool relief for those who are scorched
by anger.*

When Joseph's brothers saw that their father was dead, they said, "Perhaps Joseph will hate us, and may actually repay us for all the evil which we did to him."

—GEN. 50:15

Police in Eureka, Montana, used a backhoe to unearth a late model Chevy. A man had been notified that it would be repossessed. Rather than live with that on his record, he buried the car and reported it stolen. Insurance paid off the car and even left him with extra cash. But he bragged about it in a barroom card game and soon he was bragging to a judge.

Joseph's brothers thought that they had buried their bitterness and sibling rivalry when they sold Joseph to a caravan heading south to Egypt. Yet when they stood before him some thirteen years later, their conversation reveals that they were still haunted by the ghost of guilt (Gen. 42:21–22). After their father's death, they are terrified that Joseph will exact his revenge.

Emotions like grief, bitterness, remorse, regret, hatred, and anger cannot be buried alive. Is there a broken relationship that you have tried to bury and forget about? Is there someone you need to call today and ask forgiveness from? Are you bitter and plotting revenge against someone who hurt you? Don't just bury the past—deal with it.

Father, search me for any impure attitudes and broken relationships so that I might stand before you with a clear conscience.

PROMISES TO FAMILY

Let no corrupt word proceed out of your mouth,
but what is good for necessary edification, that it
may impart grace to the hearers. —EPH. 4:29

You big dummy," she shouted. "I hate you. You're so stupid. I'm never going to play with you again." "Oh yeah?" he retorted. "You're just a selfish pig. All you ever think about is yourself. You're not the only one who lives in this house."

"Where in the world did they learn to treat each other like dirt?" you ask yourself. Then the realization stabs like a knife in the heart. "From me! They are merely repeating words and phrases I have used."

We are our children's role model for interpersonal relationships. Rather than sarcastic compliments, caustic humor, or veiled barbs, we need to consciously reshape our words and tone of voice to be constructive, not destructive. Our conversations should appear more like brick, mortar, and trowel rather than a wrecking ball.

Father, help me to put my brain in gear before I engage my mouth in conversation.

*A merry heart does good, like medicine, but a
broken spirit dries the bones.*

—PROV. 17:22

In the midst of working at home one morning, Sam's two daughters came downstairs, looked him in the eye, and said whiningly, "Dad, we want you to play with us." Their tone of voice and the glassy look in their eyes told him that their emotional bank accounts were woefully overdrawn. Turning off the computer, he told them that what they both needed was a tickle vitamin. For the next hour, they wrestled, tickled, rocked, played "lion," gave piggy-back rides, growled and screamed at each other. By lunchtime, a smile was back on their faces, the bounce returned to their steps, and "Mr. Whine" had been banished outside once again. For the next couple of hours, they would be able to draw from the deposit made into their accounts.

Laughter, humor, and physical touch refresh the spirit far more than a lecture or a stern look. The face lightens up, the shoulders straighten, and the step becomes more lively. When the emotional bank account receives a substantial deposit, it can't help but be reflected on the face.

Father, help me deposit a sense of outrageous joy into my children's account today.

Hope deferred makes the heart sick, but when the desire comes, it is a tree of life. —PROV. 13:12

Dad," said Johnny for the fourteenth time, "when are we going to go to the park and fly my kite? You promised we would go when the weather cleared up. Can we go now? Please can we go? Please?"

Sam had been putting his son off for the past month. The first weekend, he was out of town on a business trip. The next weekend, he went hunting with the guys from the club. The weekend after that it was raining. And now, another weekend was looming on the horizon. But if it was clear, he was really hoping to go play golf with his brother-in-law.

"I don't know, Son," he replied. "We'll just have to see. I promise you we'll go sometime."

When a child's hopes and dreams are constantly ignored or put off, they eventually diminish and disappear. They become cynical and pessimistic about the promises of others, especially adults. But when promises are kept and hope is rewarded, optimism is fueled and hope grows ever larger and stronger.

Father, help me to keep my word to my children so that their hope and trust will grow.

Though He slay me, yet will I trust Him.
—JOB 13:15

The last four years of his life, Jake's father could have written the book of Job. A damaged optic nerve in one eye and a blood clot behind the other eye left him legally blind. His car was struck by a train at a faulty crossing guard, leaving him with a broken shoulder and broken hip. Months of recovery and rehabilitation preceded his return to work. Diagnosed with cancer in April, he died in December. Four years of pain, heartache, and questions, including "Why, God?"

In one of their last meetings, Jake asked him what he thought about during these experiences. How had it affected his faith in God? Did he ever question what God was doing? What were his plans for the future? What lessons had he learned in the process?

Expecting bitterness, confusion, or rejection, Jake was surprised by his father's quiet confidence in God's sovereignty. He clung tenaciously to the belief that God was in control and would do what was best for him.

_____

Father, help me to leave my children a legacy of hope and trust in you that does not waiver in the midst of circumstances too difficult to understand.

Husbands, love your wives, just as Christ also loved the church and gave Himself for it.

—EPH. 5:25

Don typically arose early on Saturday mornings to either play eighteen holes of golf or three sets of tennis with his buddies. After a grueling match on the greens or the court, he would retire in front of the TV to watch whatever game was on. His idea of heaven was anything that included a ball.

But when his wife, Sharon, would ask him to take her shopping at the mall, he would complain about how his back hurt, how much work he had to do, or how far behind he was on his projects in the garden. On those rare occasions when she prevailed on his sense of guilt, he imagined a sign hanging over the entrance to the store, "Abandon all hope ye who enter here."

Christ's command to love our wives means that we repeatedly face the call to die to self for the sake of our wives. If we truly love our wives we will forsake the gentle rolling greens or the clay courts for the fiery gates of the mall because we value their interests and love to be with them. Sacrificial love dies to self and willingly serves the one it loves in unsung domestic heroism. It doesn't even demand a medal or record a point scored.

Father, help me to willingly serve my wife without complaint.

*Husbands, love your wives, just as Christ also loved
the church and gave Himself for it, that He might
sanctify and cleanse it with the washing of water
by the word, that He might present it to Himself a
glorious church, not having spot or wrinkle or any
such thing, but that it should be holy and without
blemish.*
—EPH. 5:25–27

Peter spent hours each weekend working on his new
truck. He washed, waxed, and buffed it until it was brilliant. And he would not allow anyone to touch the
body or lean on the fenders for fear of scratching it—
he even made people sit on a towel rather than directly
on the upholstery.

Transfer that same picture to how you demonstrate
your love for your wife in regard to her spiritual growth
and maturity. As she moves through life, she grows to
be more like Jesus Christ and to reflect his character.
While her salvation and sanctification are solely due
to the work of Christ, you are a humble partner in developing her inner beauty and luster.

In order to have this kind of effect, we must periodically ask ourselves the tough questions, "Is my wife
more godly because she is married to me? Or is she
more godly in spite of me? What can I do to encourage
her to grow and mature in her relationship to Christ?"

Father, help me to have a positive impact on my wife's spiritual life.

*So husbands ought to love their own wives as their
own bodies; he who loves his wife loves himself.*
—EPH. 5:28

Jeremy arose at 5:00 A.M. every morning to go jogging. When he returned, he would do several repeti-
tions of pushups and situps. Before taking his shower,
he would examine himself in the mirror. Stomach flat
enough? Any sign of fat? Muscle tone evident? Following a healthy breakfast, he would head for the office.

Over lunch one day with Jayson, Jeremy admitted
that his marriage was struggling. "Did you ever think
about directing the same diligent attitude toward your
marriage that you do to staying in shape physically?"
Jayson asked gently. "You are always in tune with how
tight your muscles are; are you equally aware of how
tight your wife's emotions are? Didn't you spend $100
on jogging shoes because they absorbed the shock of
the road better? How much do you invest to reduce
the shock of life on your wife?" Jayson continued, "You
know, it takes as much, or more, work to train for a
lifetime of marriage as it does to run a marathon. Why
not develop a plan for her growth?"

*Lord, remind me that my wife is a vital part of my life, and that I
need to care for her.*

"And he arose and came to his father. But when he was still a great way off, his father saw him and had compassion, and ran and fell on his neck and kissed him."
—LUKE 15:20

I couldn't believe my parents' response," explained Steve. "What they did just blew my socks off. I thought they would kill me, not welcome me back with open arms. It was the last thing I thought they would do."

As a sixteen-year-old, Steve felt unloved and unwanted. Adopted as a baby, he never really thought his adopted parents loved him. Whenever there was a fight at home, he always blamed himself. "They would be better off without me," he often said to himself.

One Sunday afternoon, he decided he'd had enough. Leaving his home, he hitchhiked to his best friend's house, fifteen miles away. He left his parents a brief note explaining he was leaving and never coming back.

Eight hours and a change of heart later, Steve fearfully opened the front door. Anticipating a tongue lashing, a beating, or being grounded, he was not prepared for what he found. His parents were on their knees praying for him! For the first time in his life, he felt loved and accepted.

Father, help me to communicate unconditional love, acceptance, and forgiveness to my children.

*Just as He chose us in Him before the foundation
of the world, that we should be holy and without
blame before Him in love, having predestined us
to adoption as sons by Jesus Christ to Himself,
according to the good pleasure of His will.*
—EPH. 1:4–5

George grew up as an adopted child, the older of two
boys. A short time after receiving George, Betty became pregnant. Fourteen months after adopting
George, Tom was born.

Twenty years later as students in college, Tom ran
across Ephesians 1:4–5 and was struggling to understand the concept of adoption. "George," he asked his
brother, "what did it feel like to be adopted?" "I don't
know," George replied. "I never felt adopted. I always
felt like I was part of the family."

Just as legal adoption makes one a full-fledged member of the family with all the rights and privileges of
an heir, so adoption into God's family makes us joint
heirs with all other believers—we are welcomed into
the very family of God.

*Father, as you joyfully accept me into your family, help me to roll
out the welcome mat for your children. Help me to communicate that
I love them.*

MARCH

Promises You Make
to Others

*Nevertheless God, who comforts the downcast,
comforted us by the coming of Titus.*

—2 COR. 7:6

Six-year-old Billy was about to embark on his maiden voyage on a bicycle. As he prepared to cast off, his older brother Bobby held on to the handle bars. As the bicycle started down the sidewalk, his mom and dad cheered proudly. Bobby ran alongside, steadying the bike and shouting instructions to his brother. After twenty yards, Bobby let go. Billy kept going on his own power, his face beaming. After a few more yards, the bike began to teeter and wobble. At that point, Bobby's friend, Matt, was waiting. He too ran alongside, steadying the bicycle and cheering the rider. Billy accomplished a major goal: riding a two-wheeler.

The Greek word for comfort is *parakaleo*. It has a wide range of meanings which include "beg, request, appeal, comfort, cheer up." It literally means, "call alongside." It is the same word which serves as one of the titles of the Holy Spirit, the "Paraclete": the one who comes alongside in order to help.

As believers, we are called to come alongside other believers in order to comfort, challenge, and encourage them. It is what Kent Hughes refers to as *"The Titus Touch—the golden touch of an encouraging friend."*[2]

Father, bring me to people who need encouragement and allow me to comfort them.

PROMISES TO OTHERS

And let us consider one another in order to stir up love and good works.
—HEB. 10:24

The process of encouragement means to direct one's mind and interest toward something. It begins with examining, or considering, the other person. We need to be students of each other, intently analyzing and paying attention to each other's needs.

As we talk with one another, we need to pay attention to the words, the emotions behind those words, and body language. Rather than frame a reply, we need to concentrate on understanding what is said and meant.

John spoke with me many times about his desire to have deep, satisfying friendships. But after talking to him, I was always puzzled. Reflecting on our conversations, I noticed that his body language contradicted everything he said. I asked him about his behavior. "John, do you realize that every time we talk, you keep your hands in your pockets and you always look at the ground? If you tried to make eye contact, you would encourage people to talk more."

Lord, help me to be a student of people and learn to observe in order to meet their needs.

. . . but exhort one another daily, while it is called "Today," lest any of you be hardened through the deceitfulness of sin.
                                                        —HEB. 3:13

When lifting rough objects like wood or concrete, we wear gloves to prevent our hands from becoming cut and callused. In the same way, when surrounded by evil and sin, encouragement prevents our heart from becoming hardened, callused, and deceived by sin.

Randy met with Sam to talk with him about his recent behavior. "Sam, in the past six weeks you have alienated everyone around you. You have great potential for leadership and ministry, but your anger is a millstone around your neck. You have to learn to control your anger before it destroys you. And we think you can do it and we want to help you conquer this giant."

In light of the fact that Jesus Christ is coming back soon, we are called to encourage one another. It is to be our daily habit. Rather than whining, complaining, or commiserating with each other about how bad life is, we are to examine, encourage, and excite each other.

Father, help me to be willing to confront a friend to prevent him from developing a callused attitude toward you.

*And let us consider one another in order to stir up
love and good works, not forsaking the assembling
of ourselves together, as is the manner of some, but
exhorting one another, and so much the more as
you see the Day approaching.* —HEB. 10:24–25

Jan stopped by the church looking for the title of a
song. Her grandfather had died suddenly and she
needed a copy of his favorite song for the funeral. As
they talked, the pastor put his hand on her shoulder
and softly squeezed in order to console her.

The term used for encourage, *parakaleo,* has a
broad range of meaning, everything from comfort to
confrontation. How we practice or apply it depends on
the need and the goal. Is the person soft and contrite,
or saddened and grieving? Then perhaps they merely
need comfort, a soft, gentle voice telling them we understand and hurt with them. Do they arrogantly boast
of things they have done wrong and are unwilling to
change? In this case they most likely need someone to
exhort, challenge, and contend with them until they
come to repentance.

*Lord, help me to know the needs of people in order to encourage
them properly.*

PROMISES TO OTHERS

And let us consider one another in order to stir up love and good works. —HEB. 10:24

As they rounded into the home stretch, the riders were neck and neck. It was going to be a photo finish. Which horse would win the Kentucky Derby? As they neared the finish line, the jockey in the purple silks went to the whip to encourage his mount on to victory.

The word used for "spur" generally has a negative connotation. It usually means to provoke, irritate, or exasperate. This does not give one permission to have an irritating personality and habits that exasperate other people. What it says is that encouragement will act as a sharp object to poke and prod someone into moving forward. As a jockey goes to the whip to urge his mount on to victory, so encouragement spurs someone on to love and good deeds.

In order to do this effectively, we must know and understand the person or group that we are trying to encourage. We need to comprehend what motivates them. Rather than assume that "one size fits all," we need to tailor our encouragement to the individual's needs, personality, and circumstance.

Father, help me to be a gentle poke in the side, prodding others for spiritual growth.

And let us consider one another in order to stir up love and good works, . . . but exhorting one another, and so much the more as you see the Day approaching. —HEB. 10:24–25

Laurel was the faithful caregiver for seventy-five-year-old Victor and his wife, Betsy. Because of failing health, Victor and Betsy had been separated in different nursing homes and hospitals. Laurel worked tirelessly to reunite them in a retirement center. As they waited for that day, Victor was becoming more despondent. He just wanted to "go and be with Jesus."

One morning as Laurel checked on Victor, she spoke to him about his attitude. "Victor, you don't smile as much as you used to. You used to cheer up everyone you met, but now you are depressed and gloomy. Next week when you move into your new apartment, why don't you use that as a fresh start? Instead of giving up, ask God for opportunities to encourage others. You still have so much that you can offer to others. Let's pray for one person that you can cheer up next week. What do you think?"

By the end of their conversation, Victor was filled with new hope and resolve. His future once again held some rays of sunshine.

Lord, help me to be a ray of sunshine in the lives of others.

PROMISES TO OTHERS

*So we, being many, are one body in Christ, and
individually members of one another.*

—ROM. 12:5

At a speech in Pittsburgh in July 1833, Daniel Webster, the great statesman and orator proclaimed, "There are many objects of great value to man which cannot be attained by unconnected individuals, but must be attained, if attained at all, by association." In 1965, songwriter Paul Simon penned the song "I Am a Rock." Rather than being a declaration of independence, the song was a statement that we really do need each other. As has often been pointed out, even the Lone Ranger had Tonto.

Seven out of ten adult Americans belong to at least one association, be it the PTA, a condo or homeowners association, the American Association of Retired Persons (the largest, with 33 million members), or even the International Fancy Guppy Association (among the smallest, with twenty-nine members). We have learned that we can accomplish more together than we can apart.

We need the encouragement and accountability of others who will check up on us, ask us the tough questions, and offer support. Whom do you have that provides that kind of support and encouragement?

_____

*Father, help me to open myself up to others so that we can mutually
encourage one another.*

PROMISES TO OTHERS

Be kindly affectionate to one another with brotherly love, . . .
—ROM. 12:10

Growing up, Joe always wanted to be like his older brother, Mike. If Mike joined the band, then Joe nagged his parents until they got him an instrument too. If Mike played basketball, then Joe tried to learn how to dribble and shoot hoops as well.

That doesn't mean they always agreed with each other and lived in peace. They had their share of knock-down, drag-out, roll-on-the-floor, pinch-punch brawls. But let someone criticize his brother in Joe's presence and he would be in their face.

This is the picture Paul has in mind when he basically says, *Be kindly affectionate to one another with brotherly love.* The word *devoted* refers to the loving affection, or tenderness, that exists between parents and children. Rather than live in isolation, we are part of a larger family. As a result, we are to love, protect, cherish, and honor our brothers and sisters in Christ, just as we would if we had the same father. And when you come to think of it, we do.

Father, help me to view other believers as being a vital part of my life and help me to express my tender affection to them in appropriate ways.

. . . in honor giving preference to one another.
—ROM. 12:10

The division in a certain church became so heated that one group entered into a lawsuit against the other in order to claim the church property for itself. The judge finally ruled it was not in the province of the civil courts to settle this matter if it had not first been aired before the church courts.

Eventually a church court assembled to hear both sides of the case. After lengthy discussions, the higher judiciary of the denomination awarded the church property to one of the two factions. The losers withdrew and started another church nearby. When they traced the disagreement to its source, the papers reported that the trouble began when an elder at a church dinner received a smaller slice of ham than a child seated next to him!

In contrast, Paul instructs us to honor one another. We are to have a healthy respect and a willingness to defer to each other. In light of the security that comes from knowing who we are in Christ, we are free to lift others up and to honor them.

Lord, grant me a willingness to promote the cause of others.

*Be of the same mind toward one another. Do not
set your mind on high things, but associate with the
humble. Do not be wise in your own opinion.*
—ROM. 12:16

When Fred was in junior high and senior high school,
he played trumpet and French horn in the band and
orchestra. The music played was usually divided into
parts: the first trumpets played the melody, and the
second and third trumpets played different elements
of harmony. Everyone wanted to be in the first trumpets since they were viewed as the best.

Each week they had challenges, in which you would
try to play the music better than the person sitting in
the chair above you so you could move up. You had
arrived when you made it to the first chair and became
first trumpet. (You could play melody and not waste
time with that boring harmony.)

How often we approach life with that same attitude.
We strive to be number one, to leap-frog our way to
the top of the ladder. We don't realize that it takes just
as much skill to play the harmony successfully. To do
so, however, means that we need to rein in our egos.
We must consciously remind ourselves that the contributions of others are just as valuable. Harmony adds a
much needed depth and richness and completes the
music.

*Lord, let me listen to the tunes that others play in order to blend mine
in and be part of the symphony that you are conducting.*

PROMISES TO OTHERS

*Therefore receive one another, just as Christ also
received us, to the glory of God.* —ROM. 15:7

Mark," said Ellen, "I was really offended by the
Drama Festival yesterday. There was no Christian content at all. In fact, I was so offended that I left after
twenty minutes."

"You're kidding," countered Josh. "I invited two
non-Christian friends and they loved it. In fact, we had
a great discussion about the Bible's view of sex and
morality."

When it comes to gray areas that Scripture does not
speak clearly about, there are two possible extremes:
The legalists and the libertines. If these groups were
to go white water rafting, the legalists would avoid all
the rapids while the libertines would bump through the
rapids without a guide, get hung up on the rocks, and
possibly drown. In contrast to both, the goal should be
to circumnavigate the river in a safe fashion.

Paul's instruction in Romans 15:7 was to accept one
another. Fellowship is based on the willingness to take
someone into your heart, not on total agreement. We
may need to agree to disagree. That often brings more
praise to God than demonstrating that we are right.

*Father, help me to understand and accept those who have a different
perspective than I do.*

Greet one another with a holy kiss.
—ROM. 16:16

Hi, how are you doing?" "Fine. You?" "Fine." An empty exchange of words that masquerades as a meaningful, friendly greeting. While that should obviously be avoided, does Paul mean that we should kiss everyone we come in contact with?

Paul's instruction has puzzled many for a long time. The word *greet* literally means to embrace. This meaning is portrayed by the mutual greeting of two good friends and includes offering one's hand, embracing, kissing, and bowing the knee to serve. This form of greeting is still common in many Middle Eastern and eastern European countries.

The key principle is that a greeting should be a true expression of concern and love. Whether or not we do it physically, we need to embrace people emotionally and welcome them into our hearts.

Father, help me to radiate warmth to those I come in contact with.

PROMISES TO OTHERS

Be hospitable to one another without grumbling.
—1 PETER 4:9

General Robert E. Lee was riding on a train to Richmond. The general was seated at the rear, and all the other places were filled with officers and soldiers. A poorly dressed elderly woman entered the coach at one of the stations. Having no seat offered to her, she trudged down the aisle to the back of the car. Immediately, Lee stood up and gave her his place. One man after another then arose to give the general his seat. "No, gentlemen," he said, "if there is none for this lady, there can be none for me!"

For some reason, we think we are hospitable when we have our friends over for dinner. However, the true idea of hospitality is to entertain strangers. This requires that we be willing to open up our homes and resources to the needs of others, even those we deem beneath us.

Being a Christian, General Lee knew that good manners and humility demand consideration for people in all walks of life, not merely for those of high social ranking like himself.

Father, help me to use what I have to meet the needs of others.

With all lowliness and gentleness, with
longsuffering, bearing with one another in love.
—EPH. 4:2

While Abraham Lincoln had many enemies, no one treated him with more contempt and disrespect than Edwin Stanton. He denounced Lincoln's policies and called him a "low, cunning clown." Stanton nicknamed Lincoln "the original gorilla" and said that explorer Paul Du Chaillu was foolish to wander about in Africa trying to capture a gorilla, when he could have found one so easily in Springfield, Illinois! While it would have been natural to retaliate, Lincoln said nothing in reply. In fact, he went to the other extreme and made Stanton his Minister of War because Stanton was the best man for the job.

The fateful night came when Lincoln was struck down by an assassin's bullet in Ford's Theater. In a room off to the side, where Lincoln's body was taken, Stanton stood and looked down on the silent, rugged face of the president. Through his tears, he said, "There lies the greatest ruler of men the world has ever seen." The patience of love had conquered in the end.

Lord, rather than try to get even, help me to put up with and be patient with those who irritate me.

MARCH 15

And be kind to one another, tenderhearted, ...
—EPH. 4:32

When Clare Boothe Luce, then seventy-five, was asked, "Do you have any regrets?" she answered: "Yes, I should have been a better person. Kinder. More tolerant. Sometimes I wake up in the middle of the night, and I remember a girlhood friend of mine who had a brain tumor and called me three times to come and see her. I was always too busy, and when she died, I was profoundly ashamed. I still remember that after fifty-six years."

In contrast is a family who guides a ministry for people who suffer from Down's Syndrome. Twice a month, they host a dinner and game night for this group. They recruit their family members and friends, prepare a sumptuous meal, organize games in the gym, and have a separate meeting for the parents so that they may support and encourage each other. Through their attitudes, actions, and lifestyle, they demonstrate a heart of kindness and compassion.

Father, help me to be kind and gentle to those I come in contact with.

. . . forgiving one another, as God in Christ also forgave you.
                                              —EPH. 4:32

A wealthy English merchant who lived on the European continent was satisfied with nothing but the finest things in life. He had owned a Rolls-Royce coupe for years and it had provided him with great service all that time. One day, while driving down a bumpy road, his car hit a deep pothole, resulting in a broken rear axle.

He immediately shipped the car back to the Rolls plant in England and was not surprised by the quick repair that was performed. However, he was surprised that he did not receive a bill even though the warranty had run out. He waited for months and still no bill came. He finally communicated with the company about the bill for his car repairs. The factory again responded quickly and said, "We have thoroughly searched our files and find no record of a Rolls-Royce axle ever breaking."

The integrity and excellence of the company would not permit a flaw in workmanship or materials to be made known. The excellence of Christ does not allow our flaws to be made known to the Father. He accomplishes our forgiveness. Having received this kind of forgiveness, we should forgive the flaws of others all the more.

Father, help me to have a heart that forgives others.

PROMISES TO OTHERS

Submitting to one another in the fear of God.
—EPH. 5:21

The story is told of an eleventh-century German king, King Henry III, who grew weary of court life and the pressures of being a monarch, so he applied to a monastery to be accepted for a life of contemplation. During an interview, the religious superior of the monastery asked the king, "Your Majesty, do you understand that the pledge here is one of obedience? That will be hard because you have been a king."

Henry replied, "I understand. The rest of my life I will be obedient to you, as Christ leads you."

"Then I will tell you what to do," said the holy man. "Go back to your throne and serve faithfully in the place where God has placed you."

Like King Henry, we too often tire of our role and responsibility and need to be reminded that God has placed each of us in a particular place to be faithful there.

Lord, help me to have an attitude that says "Yes!" to your instructions.

. . . all of you be submissive to one another, and be clothed with humility, for "God resists the proud, but gives grace to the humble."   —1 PETER 5:5

An ardent music lover unexpectedly met the great Johannes Brahms. On recognizing the composer the man asked, "Master, would you please write here a small portion of a masterpiece and sign it so I can have a precious memory of this fortunate encounter?"

Brahms took the pencil and paper, and scribbled out the initial bars of "The Blue Danube" by Johann Strauss. He signed: "Unfortunately not by me, Johannes Brahms."

What a contrast to those today who say, "I am the greatest of all time." Peter says that in our relationships with others, we are to keep our egos in check. The picture is that of someone who changes clothes, hangs up his ego in the closet and puts on the jumpsuit or overcoat of humility. The person performs this ritual because the Father is pleased when we do.

Father, help me to clean the pride out of my closet and put in a new wardrobe of humility.

Be at peace among yourselves.
—1 THESS. 5:13

He hit me!" "Well, she wouldn't share her toys with me!" "But he called me a dummy."

Ahh, another peaceful evening at home . . .

Living in peace within the family is one of the greatest challenges of all. We can get along with coworkers and friends, but maintaining peace and tranquillity at home is sometimes like trying to nail Jell-o to the wall. The least little cross look, borrowed toy, thrown ball, strewn clothes, messy room . . . and WWIII breaks out.

The hardest part about maintaining peace is that we cannot control the responses and attitudes of our wife and children. We can only control our own, and with great difficulty at that. In order to set the pace for the family, we need to monitor our own immediate relationships. We need to admit when we're wrong, ask forgiveness, and watch our tone of voice; we need to praise instead of criticize, play games with our kids instead of yell at them, establishing firm guidelines and expectations—these and a host of other things can lay the groundwork for peaceful relationships.

Father, help me to remember that a peaceful home starts with me.

> *Now I plead with you, brethren, by the name of our Lord Jesus Christ, that you all speak the same thing, and that there be no divisions among you, but that you be perfectly joined together in the same mind and in the same judgment.*
>
> —1 COR. 1:10

Last summer, a friend of ours made a trip into Russia as part of a team of educators whose purpose was to help strengthen the Russian schools in the area of ethics and morality. The group was made up of teachers, pastors, lawyers, and even a couple of farmers. They met with atheists, communists, Protestants, Orthodox, and Catholics.

In making a presentation to the Russian educators on ethics and morality, they presented what the three major confessions (Protestant, Orthodox, and Catholic) held in common. They did this, even though it would have been very easy to maintain their individual distinctives in terms of beliefs, habits, and attitudes, rather than choose to come together under a common banner in order to reach a common goal.

There will never be complete and perfect agreement in any group because people have different values and opinions. The secret to unity is not total agreement, but rather agreeing to disagree without being disagreeable!

Lord, help me to know when to stand my ground on an issue and when to give in for the sake of unity.

PROMISES TO OTHERS

Bear one another's burdens, and so fulfill the law of Christ.
                                                    —GAL. 6:2

Since the school that Jerry's children attend is just around the corner, his wife walks over to meet the kids and bring them home. Invariably in the course of that walk their two-year-old daughter will stub her toe on a rock, trip, and skin her knees or hands. Sitting there sobbing, she will cry, "Carry me, Mommy. I hurt my leg. I don't want to walk anymore." Obligingly, she picks her up and carries her the rest of the way.

The instruction to carry each other's burdens comes in the context of restoring a fallen believer (Gal. 6:1). Somehow in the course of life, he was overtaken by sin and gave in to temptation. He stumbled badly, skinned his knees, scraped his hands until they were raw, and is lying there sobbing, discouraged and dejected. Our task, as spiritually mature people, is to restore fallen believers like him.

Like the good Samaritan, we come alongside, bind up his wounds, and carry him to safety. We walk with him, supporting him until he can walk on his own. We call him on the phone to check up on his walk with God and ask how we can help.

Father, help me not to be critical of those who fall into sin, but instead allow me to restore them to a steady walk with you.

*Therefore comfort each other and edify one
another, just as you also are doing.*
—1 THESS. 5:11

Several weeks ago, a storm blew through Adam's city, snapping trees and uprooting them from the ground. Sixteen of them fell behind his church, many on the neighbor's fence and into the pool in his backyard. This neighbor was a cantankerous, difficult man, complaining about anything and everything that the church did. Some smugly suggested that he received his just desserts. But the church's maintenance engineer decided to try to win a neighbor. He organized a crew to pull the trees out of the pool and rebuild the fence. They even split the trees for firewood and allowed the man to take as much as he wanted for his own use.

Paul instructs us to build up each other. That may involve shoring up the sagging beams of weak relationships. It may mean tearing down a fence that divides, and pouring the foundation for an open pathway of communication. It may involve hanging a door without a lock that invites openness and hospitality. In the process, you may tear down an emotional fence and build an archway of friendship.

Father, help me to put on my hard hat and work diligently at constructing stronger foundations for future friendships and relationships.

Therefore, putting away lying, each one speak truth with his neighbor, for we are members of one another.
—EPH. 4:25

"Well, it's time for your annual job review, David," said Alexander. "Tell me about your goals and your progress."

Alexander had dreaded this meeting for months. Several board members were dissatisfied with David's work habits and had been pressuring Alexander to either fire David or reassign him. Alexander realized that David's failure to perform at the level expected was in part his fault. He had not been clear enough in stating his expectations or clarifying his job description.

For several weeks, Alexander had told David how pleased he was about his performance. In reality, he was displeased but didn't have the heart to tell him. But now it was time to face the music and be blunt about what was really going on.

Rather than doling out false compliments or blatant lies, we should be truthful in our relationships with others. We owe that to them since we are all members of the body of Christ.

Father, help me to be honest with people and not avoid telling them the truth to either protect me or them from pain.

Confess your trespasses to one another, . . .
—JAMES 5:16

Son, I'm sorry that I spanked you. Dad was angry about something that happened at the office today and I took it out on you. I'm sorry. I was wrong. Will you forgive me?"

While it's painful to admit that we fail, it would be even worse to see the relationship with our kids deteriorate because they saw through Dad's hypocrisy when we wouldn't admit it.

A popular phrase several years ago was, "Love means never having to say you're sorry." While it sounds good, it's a lie that, when practiced, damages relationships. It is extremely difficult to grow up in a family where Mom or Dad is never wrong, or at least unwilling to admit their failures and that they make mistakes. It creates a false illusion of perfection that the child can never hope to attain, or it widens the gap between the perfect parent and the fallible child.

Love demands that we admit our mistakes and ask for forgiveness. It is the building block of strong relationships.

Father, help me to be honest about my failures.

PROMISES TO OTHERS

> *. . . as for me, far be it from me that I should sin*
> *against the LORD in ceasing to pray for you; . . .*
> —1 SAM. 12:23

There are times we just don't know how to pray for people. Our prayers degenerate into, "God bless . . . and protect them." Or it becomes a word association game. "Be with Sam . . . remember the last time we played golf . . . speaking of golf, I sure liked that new putter I tried last week . . . that was the same day as the wind storm which blew down those trees . . . I need to take care of the branches that fell at Mom's house . . . sure have a lot of memories in that old house . . . Let's see now, what was I praying for? Oh, yeah, my brother."

In Ephesians 3:16–19, Paul prays for three specific requests for a group of people miles away. He prays that God would strengthen them with power, he asks God to help them comprehend the height, depth, breadth, and width of God's love, and he prays that they would be filled with the fullness of God.

Keeping those requests in mind allows us to pray specifically for anyone regardless of whether or not we know their specific needs right now.

God, strengthen my commitment to pray for others.

A man who has friends must himself be friendly, but there is a friend who sticks closer than a brother.
—PROV. 18:24

Jerry's five-year high school reunion was scheduled to be held at Doheny State Beach on a Sunday afternoon in mid-July. He could hardly wait. He and his old classmates were going to have a great time exchanging stories about their lives. What career were they in? Who married whom? Who had kids? Who had moved away? These and countless other questions would be exchanged and answered that afternoon.

Wanting to make sure he found the place, he arrived thirty minutes early. No sign of anyone. They must be on their way. For the next two hours, he walked up and down the beach, searching in vain for a friendly face, looking for the old school sign and mascot, anything that looked familiar. But everywhere he went, the faces were the same, strangers.

Discouraged and dejected, he drove home, called up his best friend from college, and went out and talked for several hours.

Lord, help me to demonstrate commitment and loyalty in my friendships.

Then Jonathan and David made a covenant,
because he loved him as much as his own soul.
—1 SAM. 18:3

At the age of twenty, Anne Sullivan faced the daunting task of serving as tutor for the blind and deaf seven-year-old Helen Keller. At that point, Helen could only utter animal-like sounds and often fell into destructive rages. For several weeks, Anne Sullivan tried in vain to break through to the girl's consciousness. Finally, on April 5, 1887, Helen was holding a mug under the spout while Anne pumped water into it with one hand and used her other hand to repeatedly spell w-a-t-e-r. Suddenly, Helen understood!

Throughout her life, Anne Sullivan remained by her side, pouring her life into Helen's. She was satisfied to be Helen's friend and encourager, and to help her become one of the most famous women the world has ever known.

As the king's son and heir to the throne, Jonathan watched as the shepherd boy donned his robe and armament. From that point on, he no longer looked on David as a lowly shepherd, but he placed him by his side as an equal. The deepest of friendships have in common the desire to make the other person royalty. They work for and rejoice in the other's promotion, elevation, and achievements.

Father, help me to love my friends enough in order to lift them up and make them successful.

PROMISES TO OTHERS

*Open rebuke is better than love carefully
concealed. Faithful are the wounds of a
friend, but the kisses of an enemy are deceitful.*
—PROV. 27:5–6

How could they do this to me?" Tom asked himself over and over again. "They said they were my friends. Well, if this is friendship, I sure hope I don't have any enemies."

At his annual review, Don and Dennis, Tom's supervisors and closest friends, informed him that he would not be receiving a raise this year. The board of directors was displeased with his performance, and this was their signal to get his act together or he would be gone. Three months later, the board asked for Tom's resignation.

Three years later, Tom admitted that it was the best thing for him. "At the time, I felt betrayed and rejected. But it forced me to take a hard look at myself. I realized they were right—I needed to grow and develop as a leader. Once I recovered from the initial shock and learned some lessons, I discovered that being fired turned out to be the best thing for me. Even though it drove a wedge in our relationship at the time, Don and Dennis sincerely cared and wanted to help me be successful, even if it was not with their company."

Father, help me care enough to confront.

PROMISES TO OTHERS

Do not lie to one another, . . .
—COL. 3:9

W hy didn't he tell me the truth?" Dan asked Bob. "If I knew, I might have given him the time off. But now, I'm not sure I will ever trust him again. Every time he calls in sick, I'll wonder if he's telling the truth. If he had only been honest, things might be different."

Terry, an employee, had called in sick two weeks ago. Since he was a dependable worker, no one questioned him. But Bob, who promised his son he would run past the baseball stadium to buy tickets for next week's game, saw Terry enter the gate for an afternoon game. When he asked him about it later, Terry tried to deny he was there. But when a baseball pennant and the ticket stubs fell out of his locker, he was caught in the act. And it all took place in the presence of his boss, Dan. Now, his reputation was damaged and his integrity harmed.

The cliché is often tossed out, "Honesty is the best policy. That way you don't have to remember what story you told."

Father, help me to always tell the truth.

Speaking to one another in psalms and hymns and spiritual songs, singing and making melody in your heart to the Lord, . . .

—EPH. 5:19

I just don't know what I'm going to do," whined Ted for the ninth time. "I can't even find a temporary job. I've been fired twice in the last eighteen months. My roommates keep moving out on me. What am I going to do? How am I going to survive this crisis?"

Ted had developed a reputation as a whiner and complainer. He never smiled but wore a perpetual frown and look of dejection and sadness. When asked how he was doing, he would reply with a litany of problems that were always someone else's fault.

The sad part was that he never made the connection that because he was draining people, they avoided him. He expected everyone to listen to his problems and to encourage him, but he never gave back. Rather than speak words of praise and encouragement, his theme song was "Woe is me." He developed the reputation of being a black hole—one who sucked the life and energy from everyone who encountered him.

Father, help me to have a song of praise in my heart and to build up those around me.

PROMISES TO OTHERS

My brethren, do not hold the faith of our Lord
Jesus Christ, the Lord of glory, with partiality.
                                    —JAMES 2:1

Grant's church was beginning a ministry to people suffering from AIDS. At the initial planning session, an expert on this type of ministry was going to be present to speak to the group about the *Dos* and *Don'ts* of such a task. The catch was that the person who was coming had AIDS.

As he drove to the meeting, Grant struggled with what his response would be. "How should I address this individual? Would I shake hands with this person? Would I sit next to him? Would I pry into his lifestyle, demanding to know how he contracted the disease? How would I react if he volunteered that information? Is this a ministry that I should be involved in personally?" These questions and countless others were swirling through his mind.

As he pondered these issues, he was reminded of James 2:1 and the fact that favoritism is sin. The issue is not whether the distinction is made over economic, social, educational, physical, spiritual, or health concerns or differences. The issue is that our motives for making the distinction are immediately called into question because favoritism is sin.

Father, help me to see life and people through your eyes and to treat them as you would.

APRIL

Deciding to Hope
and Praise

*Because, although they knew God, they did not
glorify Him as God, nor were thankful . . .
Therefore God also gave them up to uncleanness,
in the lusts of their hearts, . . .* —ROM. 1:21, 24

Sam was a rough, irascible man who rarely acknowledged the contributions of those around him. Whenever a project was turned in to him, he would grunt unintelligibly in the direction of the person who handed it to him. After reading the report, he would nod at the person, but would rarely comment on what he read, whether good, bad, or indifferent. His coworkers never remembered him ever saying a simple "Thank you."

For most men, gratitude does not come naturally. What does come naturally is ingratitude. According to the apostle Paul, the root of rebellion is not a clenched fist toward God—a desire to do one's own thing, but rather an attitude of ingratitude. It is an unwillingness to admit that we didn't do it on our own. It is a reluctance to acknowledge our dependence on others.

When was the last time you said, "Thank you"?

Father, help me to have a heart that says, "Thank you."

Finally, brethren, whatever things are true,
whatever things are noble, whatever things are just,
whatever things are pure, whatever things are
lovely, whatever things are of good report, if there
is any virtue and if there is anything praiseworthy—
meditate on these things.

—PHIL. 4:8

Garbage in, garbage out: you are what you eat. As a man thinks in his heart, so is he. There is a direct relationship between what we put in and what comes out.

If I spend all my time listening to the complaints of critical people, I will begin to believe that everything is bad and we are doomed. If I fill my mind with evil, I should not be surprised when I act that way as well. If I want my life characterized by a positive, joyful outlook, I need to reprogram the input I allow my mind to focus on. I must be selective in choosing mental input that will build up and encourage me. If I want to be thankful, I need to focus on items that cause me to praise.

What are you filling your mind with?

Lord, help me to make wise choices in what I allow my mind to dwell on.

Hope deferred makes the heart sick, but when the desire comes, it is a tree of life. —PROV. 13:12

Jonathan was ready to give up. Every time he asked his parents for a trip to the park, a new bike, a story read to him, or for them to attend his baseball games or school activities, they would faithfully promise they would. But something always came up that prevented them from fulfilling their commitment. On one occasion, he sat on the front porch for three hours, waiting for Dad because he had said he would be home early to take him to the park. Eventually, he ate dinner and went to bed, and still no Dad. After a couple of years, he no longer had confidence in what his parents said.

In his book *Man's Search for Meaning*, Victor Frankl, successor of Sigmund Freud in Vienna, argued that the "loss of hope and courage can have a deadly effect on man." As a result of his experiences in a Nazi concentration camp, Frankl contended that when a man no longer possesses a motive for living, no future to look toward, he curls up in a corner and dies. "Any attempt to restore a man's inner strength in camp," he wrote, "had first to succeed in showing him some future goal."

Father, help me to fulfill my promises to my children and not disappoint their trust.

*So shall the knowledge of wisdom be to your soul;
if you have found it, there is a prospect, and your
hope will not be cut off.* —PROV. 24:14

Many years ago, a hydroelectric dam was to be built across a valley in New England. The people in a small town in the valley were to be relocated because the town itself would be submerged when the dam was finished. During the time between the decision to build the dam and its completion, the buildings in the town, which previously were kept up nicely, fell into disrepair. Instead of remaining a picturesque little town, it became an eyesore.

Why did this happen? The answer is simple. As one resident said, "Where there is no faith in the future, there is no work in the present."

One of the benefits of acquiring wisdom is the certain hope it gives us for the future. In addition, it provides us with the necessary motivation to live in the present in light of that certain hope. Hope provides the challenge to go on.

Father, help me to place my hope in you.

Why are you cast down, O my soul? And why are you disquieted within me? Hope in God; for I shall yet praise Him, the help of my countenance and my God.

—PS. 42:11

For the past few years, a friend has maintained the discipline of journaling. His practice ranges from several times a day to once every ten days. He records answers to prayers, written prayers, observations on his personal Bible study, and his reactions and feelings about the events of life.

He explains that he writes in it for two reasons: one is to not forget the things that God has done in his life. He wants to remind himself of how God has delivered him, answered his prayers, and stretched his faith. The second reason is to have a tool to pull him out of depression. When he gets discouraged and doubts swirl in his mind, the journey reminds him of the good gifts that God has given. It sparks and reignites the flame of his faith. By rereading it, he tells himself, *"Put your hope in God, for I will yet praise him, my Savior and my God."*

———————

Father, help me to not forget what you have done in my life.

*I will extol You, my God, O King; and I will bless
Your name forever and ever. Every day I will bless
You, and I will praise Your name forever and ever.*
—PS. 145:1–2

Several years ago, a boat was wrecked in a storm on
Lake Michigan at Evanston, Illinois. Students from
Northwestern University formed themselves into rescue teams. One student, Edward Spencer, saved seventeen people from the sinking ship. When he was
carried, due to exhaustion, to his room, he asked, "Did
I do my best? Do you think I did my best?"

Years later, R. A. Torrey was talking about this incident at a meeting in Los Angeles, when a man in the
audience called out that Edward Spencer was present.
Dr. Torrey invited him to the platform. As the audience
applauded, an old man with white hair slowly climbed
the steps. Asked by Dr. Torrey if anything in particu-
late stood out in his memory, Spencer replied, "Only
this, sir. Of the seventeen people I saved, not one of
them thanked me."

In Psalm 145, David does not say that he feels thankful. Instead, he chooses to give thanks and to praise
God.

*Father, help me to make the choice to be thankful today and to give
you praise.*

*Jesus Christ is the same yesterday, today, and
forever.*
—HEB. 13:8

A man stopped by the studio of his old friend, a music
teacher. After greeting him heartily, he said to him,
"What's the good word today?" The old teacher was
silent as he stood up and walked across the room,
picked up a hammer, and struck a tuning fork. As the
note sounded out through the room, he said, "That is
A. It is A today; it was A five thousand years ago, and
it will be A ten thousand years from now. The soprano
upstairs sings off-key, the tenor across the hall flats on
his high notes, and the piano downstairs is out of tune."
He struck the note again and said, "That is A, my
friend, and that's the good news for today."

Like the A note, the good news about God is that he
does not change. While his ways of dealing with people have changed down through history, he, himself,
has not changed in his character. He is still the loving,
creative, powerful, all-knowing, holy, merciful God
that he was when he created the world, and he will
remain that way through eternity. That's the good
news about God for today and forever.

*Father, thank you for the confidence I can have in you knowing that
you do not change.*

Oh, taste and see that the LORD is good; blessed is the man who trusts in Him!
—PS. 34:8

There is nothing more unsettling than being served food you don't recognize. A myriad of thoughts swirl through your mind. "What is this stuff anyway? How do I graciously try a little bite without offending my host? What if I don't like it? What is this sauce hiding? What if I'm allergic to something in here? Can I just eat my salad and pretend I'm not hungry?"

You gingerly dip your fork into the strange concoction and bravely put the morsel into your mouth. "Hey, this isn't so bad after all. You know what, it's really quite good. I like this."

Food cannot be enjoyed without tasting it. You must personally experience the flavors on your tongue in order to discover what they taste like. Without taking a spoonful, you'll never discover the sheer pleasure of the delightful mixture.

In the same way, you cannot sit back and stare at God and conclude he is good, bad, or indifferent. You must allow him to work in your life in order to experience him. When you do that, you discover the pleasure of his presence, the joy that he brings. You taste and discover that he is good.

Father, thanks for the joy that you bring.

Being confident of this very thing, that He who has begun a good work in you will complete it until the day of Jesus Christ.
                                                    —PHIL. 1:6

Recently, Dan's cars have been in the shop more often than they have been in his garage. Tires, shocks, struts, transmission, battery, tune-up, fuel injectors—you name it, it's been replaced or repaired.

While all the repairs were more than he could afford, the transmission repair would have broken the bank—but it didn't cost him a dime. Fortunately, it was under warranty and the manufacturer replaced it without charge. The warranty proved reliable and saved him from a great unexpected cost.

A far more reliable warranty is one which Paul speaks of in Philippians 1:6. Once God begins to work in our lives, he will not stop until we stand in his presence. He relentlessly and tirelessly works in our lives. Like a sculptor working on a statue, he fashions and shapes our character so that it will resemble the model, Jesus Christ. He will not stop work until he can see his image in our lives.

Father, thanks for the confidence that I can have in you.

*Therefore by Him let us continually offer the
sacrifice of praise to God, that is, the fruit of
our lips, giving thanks to His name.* —HEB. 13:15

You have a clear voice. Please use it. You are a big
girl now and big girls don't whine. Please talk clearly.
Use your pretty voice. OK?"

How many times has that been said to kids? If
there's one thing that drives parents crazy, it's a whining voice. Do you ever wonder how many times God
wants to tell us the same thing?

How praise could be a sacrifice may seem a puzzle.
But it's really quite simple—in order to praise God, we
must sacrifice our own agenda. Rather than greedily
beg for more, we graciously thank him for his bounti-
ful provisions. Instead of whining about how bad life is,
we choose to lift up and exalt God's character. Before
complaining about how little time we have to get
everything done, we take some of that time to willingly bow before the Father and praise him for the gift
of time. We willingly sacrifice some of our time to offer
a public declaration of the goodness and greatness of
God.

*Lord, help me to choose to praise you today for your character and
your conduct.*

HOPE & PRAISE

*I will worship toward Your holy temple, and praise
Your name for Your lovingkindness and Your truth;
for You have magnified Your word above all Your
name.*

—PS. 138:2

Most people are convinced that they should praise
God. The problem is that they don't always know what
to praise him for, or when and where to do it. Psalm
138 can help.

From David, we can learn that there is a public ele-
ment in praise. He praises God in the temple (v. 2), and
before the "gods" (v. 1). The kings of the earth will
hear of his praise (v. 4). David's praise revolves around
two things, God's attributes and his actions. He praises
God for his greatness and his grace, his loftiness and
his love, his majesty and his mercy. He gives thanks
for who God is and what he has done.

Perhaps this acrostic will help the next time you
want to praise God:

*P*ublicly
*R*emembering the
*A*ttributes and Actions of the
*I*ncomparable
*S*overeign God of
*E*ternity

---

*Father, cause me to tell others about who you are and what you have
done in my life.*

APRIL 12

*I will praise You with my whole heart; before the
gods I will sing praises to You.*

—PS. 138:1

Business and sales executives state that people world-
wide listen to the same radio station, WIIFM—"What's
In It For Me?" Before signing on the dotted line, we
want to know what the benefits are for a product or
service.

The same question needs to be asked concerning
the activity of praise and thanksgiving. What are the
benefits of praise?

Psalm 138 answers this query by describing a pro-
gression that starts with praise. David's personal praise
of God (vv. 1–3) is like a rock dropped in a pond. The
ripples spread out until they touch and are picked up
by the surrounding kings (vv. 4–5). As a group, they
join together in thanksgiving. This verbal declaration
and reminder of who God is and what he has done
strengthens the faith and confidence of those who
hear (vv. 6–8). Therefore personal praise leads to
group worship which leads to increased trust and confidence in God.

*Father, as I listen to the praise of others, cause me to join in and
declare what you have done for me.*

I will praise You with my whole heart; . . . All the
kings of the earth shall praise You, O LORD, . . .
The LORD will perfect that which concerns me.
                                    —PS. 138:1, 4, 8

Yesterday, we looked at the benefits of choosing to praise God. What if we decide not to join in the chorus? What happens if we choose ingratitude instead of thanksgiving?

When we encounter a difficult situation, rather than choose to thank God for his sovereign control and wisdom, we can complain about what has happened. "God, I don't like what you are doing in my life. This is a crummy deal and it's just not fair." This attitude leads to doubts about God's character. "God, not only do I not like what you're doing, I'm not sure that you're good. How can you say you're sovereign and let this happen?" Doubts ultimately lead to despair. "God, if you're not good, and if you're not in control, I'm doomed. If you don't care, who does?"

Thanksgiving leads to worship; worship leads to confidence. Ingratitude leads to doubts; doubts lead to despair. Each choice progresses to its logical conclusion. Which will you choose today: *thanksgiving* or *ingratitude?*

Father, help me to choose to say, "Thank you."

The LORD will perfect that which concerns me; Your mercy, O LORD, endures forever; do not forsake the works of Your hands.
—PS. 138:8

Early in his marriage, Dave and his wife joined a local health club. It was such a great deal that it seemed almost too good to be true! With one low initial payment, they obtained a lifetime membership with no additional cost (no monthly dues or yearly renewal). They would be in great shape physically, and financially, for the rest of their days. Plus, they could use their membership at other clubs around the country.

When the club went out of business six months later, they discovered what a lifetime guarantee really meant. It meant the club's lifetime, not theirs. It turned out that the contract wasn't worth the paper it was written on.

Fortunately, we serve a God who does not change his mind about his promises. We can be absolutely certain that God will continue to work in our lives and mold and shape us into the image of Jesus Christ. Why? Because he promised it several times in the Bible. It is a rock solid guarantee!

Father, thank you for the confidence that I can have that you will fulfill your promises.

*Let us therefore come boldly to the throne of grace,
that we my obtain mercy and find grace to help in
time of need.*   —HEB. 4:16

In Saudi Arabia, according to Arab custom, which was
reinforced by a 1952 decree of King Abdul Aziz, every
subject has the right of access to his ruler—whether
the ruler is a tribal sheik, a governor, or the monarch—
to present petitions of complaint or pleas for help.
Even the poorest Saudi can approach his sovereign to
plead a cause. Crown Prince Fahd, speaking about this
custom, said, "Anyone, anyone can come here. That
gives them confidence in their government . . . They
know they may look to us for help."

In the same way, every Christian has the right to
approach an even greater monarch, the King of Kings.
Because our high priest, Jesus, was tempted in every
way (just as we are)—yet did not sin, we have someone
who can identify with us completely. He is able to sym-
pathize with our weaknesses. As a result, we can enter
his presence, his confidence, knowing that he will not
only receive us, but will grant us the aid that we need.

Father, thank you for the open door that I have into your presence.

*For He made Him who knew no sin to be sin for
us, that we might become the righteousness of God
in Him.*
                                              —2 COR. 5:21

A Chinese Confucian scholar, converted to Christ,
told this story:

"A man fell into a dark, dirty, slimy pit, and he tried
to climb out of the pit and he couldn't. Confucius came
along. He saw the man in the pit and said, 'Poor fellow,
if he'd listened to me, he never would have got there,'
and he went on.

"Buddha came along. He saw the man in the pit and
said, 'Poor fellow, if he'll come up here, I'll help him.'
And he too went on.

"Then Jesus Christ came. He saw the man and said,
'Poor fellow!' and jumped into the pit and lifted him
out."

We serve a great God who should be praised because he was willing to send his own Son into the pit
in order to bring us out. Amazing!

*Father, thank you for how you have demonstrated your grace in
my life.*

For our citizenship is in heaven, from which we also eagerly wait for the Savior, the Lord Jesus Christ.

—PHIL. 3:20

Jonathan and Amanda had been sitting on the stairway for twenty minutes, alternately staring out the window and asking their mother, "When will Daddy be home?" They stood on their tiptoes, trying to see over their younger sister, Caitlin's, head. They wanted to catch the first glimpse of their father's car as it came around the corner and turned into the driveway.

When at last they saw it, they threw open the front door, squealed with delight, ran out on the front porch, jumped up and down, and waved with all their might. Daddy was home!

As believers, while our temporary residence is here on earth, our home is in heaven. Many years ago, Jesus left earth to go prepare heaven for our arrival. But he promised to return for us. And now, like children, we eagerly wait—standing on tiptoe, peering over the window sill into the heavens, hoping for a glimpse of his return. Soon he will be back.

Father, build a sense of anticipation within me as I wait for your return.

"I am the good shepherd. The good shepherd gives His life for the sheep."
—JOHN 10:11

Visiting a sheepfold in Switzerland, a woman discovered a sheep with a broken leg sitting next to the shepherd. Sympathetically, the woman looked inquiringly to the shepherd as she asked how it happened.

"I broke it myself," the shepherd explained. "On many occasions, this sheep wandered away to the edge of a perilous cliff. Not only was it disobedient, it was leading the other sheep astray. But now, with a broken leg, it will be forced to depend on me. I will carry it in my arms over the rivers and up the hills. I will bring him food and nourishment. In time, he will learn the valuable lesson of staying close to the shepherd."

In the same way, God sometimes breaks our hearts with the loss of a job, a relationship, a loved one, or a ministry. But what appears to be cruelty is in reality kindness. Like the shepherd, the pain is inflicted not to hurt us, but to restore. He wants us to learn to walk with and depend on him.

Father, help me to learn to rely on you and not to wander away from your side.

And everyone who has this hope in Him purifies himself, just as He is pure. —1 JOHN 3:3

B. J. Honeycutt, a character on the TV series "M.A.S.H.," was asked why he didn't give in to temptation in the midst of the Korean War. He said, "I live in an insane world where nothing makes sense. Everyone around me lives for the now, because there may not be a tomorrow. But I have to live for tomorrow, because for me there is no now."

For B. J., his hope for the future was being reunited with his wife and daughter. That hope was sufficient to define how he would behave in an extremely difficult situation.

Rather than merely provide motivation for the future, hope also has a purifying effect on one's life. It enables us to withstand temptation and say "No" to things that will compromise our values. How much more should our future hope of the kingdom of God affect how we live today?

Lord, keep my mind focused on you so that I do not give in to temptation and compromise my testimony.

APRIL 20

In this is love, not that we loved God, but that He loved us and sent His Son to be the propitiation for our sins.
—1 JOHN 4:10

As they were walking down the corridor in the office, Tom turned to his coworker Ted and said, "Ted, you always talk about how hard it is to be a dad. Sometimes it sounds like it would be better to stay single like me. Why do you love your four children?"

Ted thought for a minute, trying to come up with a profound and insightful reply. But the only answer he could come up with was "Because they're mine. Granted, sometimes they are a real handful, but I wouldn't trade them for anything. They don't have to do anything to prove themselves to me. They are my kids, and I love them."

Because of his very nature, God loves us just as we are. In the midst of our sin and rebellion, he sent Jesus to pay the penalty for our sin. He initiated the process, and we responded to his demonstration of love. Great and unmatched is his love.

Father, I am overwhelmed by the fact that you love me. Thank you.

"For with God nothing will be impossible."
—LUKE 1:37

After church one Sunday, ten-year-old Jimmy was sitting on the front steps of the church waiting for his parents to come and pick him up. Pastor Jerry saw him sitting there and tried to strike up a conversation. Knowing that the boy had just come from Sunday school, the pastor decided to try to find out what Jimmy was learning.

Pastor Jerry asked him, "Jimmy, I understand you've been learning about God in Sunday school."

"I sure have," came the earnest reply.

"Jimmy," said the pastor, "if you can tell me something that God can do, I'll give you a big shiny apple."

Jimmy pondered the question for a moment and then replied with a wisdom beyond his years, "Pastor, if you can tell me something that God can't do, I'll give you a whole box of apples."

We serve a God who delights to make the impossible possible.

Father, thank you that I can have the confidence that you can do anything.

The eyes of the LORD are on the righteous, And His ears are open to their cry.

—PS. 34:15

The story is told of an elderly grandfather who was very wealthy. Because he was going deaf, he decided to buy a hearing aid. Two weeks later, he stopped by the store where he had bought it. When asked by the manager how it was working, he replied that he could now pick up conversations quite easily, even in the next room. "Your relatives must be very pleased to know that you can hear so much better," beamed the delighted proprietor.

"Oh, they don't even know. I haven't told them yet," the man chuckled. "For the past two weeks, I've just been sitting around the house listening. But I tell you what, I've changed my will twice!"

God is not like a dear old grandfather who hears only when we speak clearly and directly to him. His ears are tuned in to our cries and we never have to shout. He always hears us. And because of his grace toward us, his attitude about us is not changed by what he hears.

Father, because you listen to me, I will call upon you every day of my life.

For by grace you have been saved . . .
—EPH. 2:8

Many years go, there was an assassination attempt of Queen Elizabeth I of England. The would-be assassin dressed as a male page and hid in the queen's boudoir, not realizing that the queen's attendants would carefully search the room. They found the woman hiding among the gowns and brought her before the queen.

Realizing her case was hopeless, she threw herself down and pleaded and begged the queen for mercy. Queen Elizabeth looked at her coldly and quietly said, "If I show you grace, what promise will you make for the future?" Looking up at the queen, she said quietly but courageously, "Grace that hath condition, grace that is fettered by precautions, is not grace at all." Realizing the truth of her comment, Queen Elizabeth replied, "You are right; I pardon you of my grace." And she went away, a free woman.

History records that the queen had no more faithful, devoted servant than the woman who had intended to take her life. In the same way, God's grace transforms us from an enemy to a faithful servant, and even beyond, to a friend.

Father, help me to respond to your grace by serving you with all my strength.

> "For God so loved the world that He gave His only
> begotten Son, that whoever believes in Him should
> not perish but have everlasting life."
>
> —JOHN 3:16

Daddy," asked the little boy, "how does God love us?" His father answered, "Unconditionally."

The lad thought for a moment. "What does unconditional mean?" After a few minutes of silence, the father replied, "Do you remember the two boys who used to live next door and the cute puppy they got last Christmas?" "Yes." "Do you recall how they used to tease it, throw sticks and rocks at it?" "Yes." "Do you remember how the puppy would always greet them with a wagging tail and would try to lick their faces?" "Yes." "Well, that puppy had unconditional love for those boys. They certainly didn't deserve his love for them because they were mean to him. But he still loved them."

The father went on to explain, "God's love for us is also unconditional. Men threw rocks at his Son, Jesus, and hit him with sticks. They even killed him. But Jesus loved them anyway."

Lord, I'm overwhelmed by your unconditional love for me. Thanks.

HOPE & PRAISE

But God, who is rich in mercy . . . even when we were dead in trespasses, made us alive together with Christ . . .
—EPH. 2:4–5

The story has been told of a mother who sought from Napoleon the pardon of her son. Because it was the young man's second offense, the emperor explained that justice demanded his death. "I don't ask for justice," said the mother. "I plead for mercy."

"But," said the emperor, "he does not deserve mercy."

"Sir," cried the mother, "it would not be mercy if he deserved it, and mercy is all I ask."

"Well, then," the emperor relented, "I will show mercy." And her son was saved.

For us, the Law demands death as the penalty of sin. But rather than give us what we deserved, God was merciful and allowed Jesus Christ to pay the penalty for us. Instead of death, we have been given life.

Father, thanks for sparing me from the fate that I deserved.

> *Blessed is the man who endures temptation; for*
> *when he has been proved, he will receive the crown*
> *of life which the Lord has promised to those who*
> *love Him.*
> —JAMES 1:12

In the New Testament, the word translated "trial" or "temptation" has two shades of meaning. When used of God's testing of man, it carries a positive intention, a desire to prove one's strengths. In contrast, when it refers to the temptation of man by Satan or another person, the word carries with it the desire to bring out one's weaknesses or bad points.

The latter idea would be like reading *Consumer Reports* before shopping for a new car. You want to find out if the car has a history of frequent repairs and equipment failure. In contrast, the first idea is demonstrated by reading the specifications put out by the automobile manufacturer. Their motivation is to point out the car's good qualities. Both serve a purpose.

In James 1:2–4, 12, the author indicates that God allows us to go through trials and testings in order to cause us to grow and ultimately receive rewards.

Father, thank you that even in trials, you have my best interests at heart.

> *"I know that You can do everything, and that no*
> *purpose of Yours can be withheld from You."*
> —JOB 42:2

Wilson Johnson, the founder of Holiday Inn motels, worked in a sawmill until the age of forty. And then one morning his life was completely changed. He explains, "When I was forty years old I worked in a sawmill. One morning the boss told me I was fired. Depressed and discouraged, I felt like the world had caved in. When I told my wife what had happened, she asked me what I was going to do. I replied, 'I'm going to mortgage our little home and go into the building business.'

"My first venture was the construction of two small buildings. Within five years I was a multimillionaire! At the time it happened, I didn't understand why I was fired. Later, I saw that it was God's unerring and wondrous plan to get me into the way of his choosing."

Lord, thanks for the confidence that nothing takes you by surprise and can be used by you for your purposes.

And the peace of God, which surpasses all understanding, will guard your hearts and minds through Christ Jesus.

—PHIL. 4:7

Phil and Tom were both cancer patients. Since they both shared the same doctor and attended the same church, they saw each other often and talked of their feelings and struggles. On one particular afternoon, they had vastly different outcomes to talk about. After two years of chemotherapy, Phil had just received a clean bill of health. "Tom, can you believe it? My cancer is in remission. The doctor doesn't even want to see me for six months. God is so good. I can't thank him enough. How are you doing?"

"That's great news, buddy," said Tom. "I am really happy for you." After a brief pause, he added, "I'm doing all right." Two weeks earlier, Tom had received news that his cancer was terminal and he had less than six months to live. He was dying and in pain. "In spite of my situation, I'm convinced that God does not make mistakes. I'd love to say that God has healed me, too. In a sense, he has, because even though I don't completely know what he's doing, he has given me peace to accept it and to trust him."

Father, give me peace and the ability to trust you especially when I don't understand.

The LORD is my rock and my fortress and my deliverer; my God, my strength, in whom I will trust; my shield and the horn of my salvation, my stronghold.
—PS. 18:2

What does a child say when he is face to face with the neighborhood bully? "My brother is bigger than your brother." "My dad is stronger than your dad." Even adults get into the act. A bumper sticker sighted on a Los Angeles freeway read, "My lawyer is better than your lawyer."

What does a three-year-old do when he gets a knot in his shoelaces? He runs to Daddy. What does a five-year-old girl do when she falls and skins her knee? She cries to Mommy for comfort.

When faced with a problem, danger, difficulty or sadness, we naturally go to someone who is bigger, stronger, and more powerful. Just as a child wants to crawl up on Daddy's lap or have Mommy's arms wrapped around him, so we go to our heavenly Father. He is the fortress that protects us from attack, the refuge that grants us asylum from persecution, the safe harbor that shelters us from the storms of life.

Father, when I face danger, let me run to your open arms for protection.

But You, O LORD, are a shield for me, my glory and the One who lifts up my head. —PS. 3:3

Seven-year-old Samantha knew she shouldn't have done it. Her daddy told her not to play by the creek. She only wanted to stand by the edge and look in, just to see the water rushing by. But she got too close, and the embankment eroded underneath her and she slipped and fell in. On the way down, she was able to grab a branch which broke her fall and prevented her from falling into the water completely. At least she only went in up to her knees. Her two older brothers, standing nearby, helped pull her out and take her home.

But the moment she had dreaded all afternoon had arrived. Dad was home from work and she had to explain why she had disobeyed. She glanced at the ground, fighting back the tears and biting her lip. But the spanking she feared most never came.

Her father, placing one hand on each side of her face, slowly raised her head until their eyes met. "I'm so glad you're safe and nothing happened," he said as he wiped the tears from her eyes.

God, having rescued us from destruction, raises our head, calms our fears, and wipes the tears from our eyes.

_____

Father, thank you for your loving care for me.

HOPE & PRAISE

MAY

Developing Wisdom and Compassion

*Happy is the man who finds wisdom, and the man
who gains understanding.* —PROV. 3:13

Wouldn't it be great if you could walk into your local
department store and buy a pound of wisdom? Or go
to a convenience store and ask for a fill-up of knowledge? Or drive through a fast-food restaurant and buy
a side order of understanding? That would be nice, but
wisdom is not so easily acquired.

Wisdom takes time and skill to acquire. Wisdom is
more than merely *knowing* right. It is more than reading and memorizing a textbook. Wisdom is actually doing right. In Hebrew, wisdom means "skill for living."
It is demonstrated in the application of knowledge. You
can read every book written on automobile mechan-
ics, but if you fill up your fuel tank with water from the
garden hose, you're not very wise. If you put oil in the
radiator or anti-freeze in the windshield washer reser-
voir, you clearly reveal a lack of understanding. We
are wise when we allow what we know to penetrate
and change our habits.

Father, help me to be skillful in using knowledge correctly.

*The things which you learned and received and
heard and saw in me, these do . . .* —PHIL. 4:9

Practice, practice, practice—you'll see successful people do it all the time. A pianist practicing scales for
thirty minutes per day. An infielder taking one hundred ground balls after baseball practice each afternoon. A football wide receiver running pass routes
over and over again. A public speaker rehearsing a
speech for the tenth time, working to get the intona-
tion and inflection of each word just right. A wood
carver checking his measurement for the second time
before making his cut. An airline pilot spending time
in a simulator. No matter what we choose to do, or
how much talent we have, we must always practice to
maintain a level of excellence.

New skills cannot be learned or existing ones mas-
tered without continued practice and rehearsal. "Use
it or lose it" is more than a catchy slogan when it
comes to maintaining a skill. It is the truth.

The truly wise person is one who continually puts
his knowledge into practice. He becomes a craftsman
in the art of applying truth to his life.

Father, continually remind me to practice what I know to be true.

The way of a fool is right in his own eyes, but he who heeds counsel is wise. —PROV. 12:15

Tom, you got a minute?" asked Ted. "I want to run this idea by you. I've tried to think through the in's and out's of the deal, but I want to get a second opinion. I remember how you caught a potential mistake on my last proposal. You sure saved my hide that time. I can't believe I misplaced that decimal point. I'd really appreciate your input on this project. Great, I'm in your debt."

After reviewing the proposal, Tom and Ted sat down to discuss the project. Tom began by saying, "From what I've seen, I think you've done your homework on this one. But have you thought about . . . ? What happens if . . . ?"

One of the marks of wisdom is the willingness to admit that you don't have all the answers. A fool shouts loudly to all around him, "Don't confuse me with the facts! I've got my mind made up!" The wise man not only seeks out advice, he listens to it, even if it may not be what he wants to hear. He is willing to admit the limitations of his knowledge and reasoning ability. He has a healthy respect for the ideas of others.

Lord, don't allow my pride to blind me to my lack of knowledge. Grant me a willingness to learn from others.

Listen to counsel and receive instruction, that you may be wise in your latter days. —PROV. 19:20

As he reflected back on his life, Jim thought how differently things might have turned out if he had not learned his lesson. As a young teenager, he had made a stupid decision about the people he ran around with. Ignoring his parents' warnings, he went out with his buddies one too many times and before he knew it, found himself behind the wheel of a stolen car.

After spending time in jail, he returned home with the vow to listen to the advice of his parents. He recognized his own flaws in judging the character of other people, especially his "friends." In light of that, he worked hard at distancing himself emotionally in order to objectively evaluate their character. When his parents pointed out the weaknesses of his friends, he tried to honestly listen rather than react defensively.

It was extremely hard at first. Sometimes he thought they were just being picky because of his past mistakes. But over time, he learned from them and discovered what they said was true. Now, thirty years later, he has developed the reputation of being a shrewd judge of character.

Father, help me to learn my lessons so that I may become wise.

WISDOM & COMPASSION

> *Whoever loves instruction loves knowledge, but he who hates reproof is stupid.* —PROV. 12:1

As a child, the thing Don hated more than anything was being punished by his parents. The sight of the "Board of Education" being taken off the kitchen wall or being put on restriction was a fate worse than death. It wasn't that his parents beat or abused him. It was just that he didn't like being told he was wrong or that he couldn't do what he wanted when he wanted.

Come to think of it, most people don't like being told they did something wrong. They hate being confronted about miscommunication and especially about character flaws. One's self-image reels when they sit across the desk from someone who points out their weaknesses.

But in spite of the pain, we should not shy away or resist such meetings. We need to realize that the other person has our best interests at heart and is merely trying to save us from ourselves. When we resist discipline, we hurt ourselves in the long run because we hinder our growth. Sometimes it means re-learning a lesson in a much more painful fashion than it should have been.

Father, give me a love for learning and a willingness to welcome discipline as a much needed friend.

*Therefore, as the elect of God, holy and beloved,
put on tender mercies, kindness, humbleness of
mind, meekness, longsuffering.*
—COL. 3:12

How would you respond if you found this ad in your local newspaper?

Clearance Sale: Special Incentive Price, One Size Fits All. A Heart of Compassion. This well-crafted garment is guaranteed to smooth out and repair broken relationships. Allows the wearer to sift through the shiny facades people put up and see the broken heart hiding under the surface. Caution: person wearing this garment may be susceptible to an occasional broken heart and a sense of being overwhelmed emotionally with the hurts of others.

Would you skim over this ad or would you call for more information? Would you be afraid to wear it? If you owned a garment of this nature, would it hang hidden away in the back of the closet or would the elbows be patched and worn thin because of constant use?

Like putting on a coat before venturing outside, Paul pictures compassion as a garment that we wear before we step into relationships with other people. In fact, he commands us to ensure that it maintains a prominent role in our daily wardrobe.

Father, help me to view people through compassionate eyes that see their pain and suffering.

WISDOM & COMPASSION

*Do not boast about tomorrow, for you do not know
what a day may bring forth.* —PROV. 27:1

A leading economic expert, Professor Irving Fisher of Yale University, made this statement about the bright future of the stock market and the American economy: "Stock prices have reached what looks like a permanently high plateau."

His statement was spoken in early October of 1929, just a couple of weeks before the stock market crash that ushered in the Great Depression. Even the so-called "recognized experts" cannot accurately predict the future.

True wisdom recognizes that all our times are in God's hands. Instead of planning our tomorrows and boasting about those plans, we would demonstrate wisdom by boasting in the God who holds the tomorrows. Boasting about what we will do sets us up for failure because we ultimately have no control of what we will do. Instead, we would be wiser to recognize our dependence on God.

Father, help me to demonstrate my reliance on you by submitting to plans and goals to your purpose and schedule.

My son, if sinners entice you, do not consent. . . .
My son, do not walk in the way with them, keep
your foot from their path.
—PROV. 1:10, 15

William Thomson (later Lord Kelvin) was one of the greatest physicists of nineteenth-century England. When he was away at college, his father wrote to him: "You are young: take care you be not led to what is wrong. A false step now, or the acquiring of an improper habit, might ruin you for life. Frequently look back on your conduct and thence learn wisdom for the future."

Dads, what kind of advice are you giving your sons and daughters? What counsel are you sharing with them that will stick with them and guide their path? What words of encouragement and wisdom will they look back on years from now and say "Thank you" for? What words of instruction have you shared will serve as bedrock, foundational principles on which they can build their life and future?

Don't minimize the power of your words and encouragement. Help your children develop a heart of wisdom.

Father, help me to share words of encouragement with my children
that will serve as guiding lights for their paths.

By pride comes only contention, but with the
well-advised is wisdom. —PROV. 13:10

One morning, the newly installed president of a bank made an appointment with his predecessor to seek some advice. He started, "Sir, as you well know, I lack a great deal of the qualifications you already have for this job. You have been very successful as president of this bank, and I wondered if you would be kind enough to share with me some of the insights you have gained from your years here that have been the keys to your success."

The older man looked at him with a stare and replied: "Young man, two words: *good decisions.*"

The young man responded, "Thank you very much, sir, but how does one come to know which is the good decision?"

"One word, young man: *experience.*"

"But how does one get experience?"

"Two words, young man: *bad decisions.*"

Father, help me to learn from my mistakes in order to gain wisdom and help me to ask for advice when I don't know the answer.

*But when He saw the multitudes, He was moved
with compassion for them, because they were
weary and scattered, like sheep having no
shepherd.*

—MATT. 9:36

As a sophomore in college, Tom's World History professor stood up and said to the class, "You have the
choice of whether or not to come to class. You can skip
all the lectures and just attend the final exam if you
like. I get paid the same amount whether you're here
or not."

During his last year of seminary, Tom's father was
dying of cancer. Partway through that fateful semester, one of his professors stopped him in the hall and
said, "You don't seem to smile as much as you used to.
Is something wrong? What's going on in your life?"

One professor couldn't care less about his students
while the other couldn't care enough. One saw his students as numbers on a page, a way to make a living
while the other saw his students as people with hurts,
concerns, and needs. One was a hired hand; the other
was a shepherd who cared about the needs of his
sheep.

Father, help me to view people with a heart of compassion.

*By pride comes only contention, but with the
well-advised is wisdom.*
                                    —PROV. 13:10

A man was on the practice golf course when the club
pro brought another man out for a lesson. The pro
watched the gentleman swing several times and
started making suggestions on how to improve his
game. Each time he offered an idea, the pupil interrupted with his own version of what was wrong and
how to correct it. After several minutes of this interfer-
ence, the pro began nodding his head in agreement.
At the conclusion of the lesson, the student paid the
pro, praising him on his expertise as a teacher, and left
in an obviously pleased frame of mind.

Astonished by this performance, the observer
turned to the golf pro and asked, "Why did you go
along with him? It was apparent he did not know what
he was doing?" "Son," the old pro said with a grin, as
he carefully pocketed his fee, "I learned long ago that
it's a waste of time to sell answers to a man who wants
to buy echoes."

When it comes to advice, do you listen to it even
when it contradicts your own ideas? Or do you merely
look for echoes?

Father, help me to listen to advice and correction.

*Wisdom is the principal thing; therefore get
wisdom. And in all your getting, get understanding.*
—PROV. 4:7

On August 11, 1978, *Double Eagle II,* a large helium
balloon, and her crew of three eased in an almost
windless sky above the potato fields of Maine. Their
destination was Paris, France. While the aerodynamics
of ballooning are somewhat complex, one thing was
certain. In order for the balloon to stay aloft as the
journey progressed, ballast, which is used to add
weight, had to be expelled. As they approached conti-
nental Europe some six days later, one of the crew
wrote in his diary, "We have been expending ballast
wisely, but as we neared land, not cheaply . . . over
went such gear as tape recorders, radios, film magazines, sleeping bags, lawn chairs, most of our water,
food, and the cooler it was in."

Next to following Christ, the pursuit of wisdom is the
wisest choice a man can make, but it does not come
cheaply. In the same way that the balloonists abandoned many important things that weighed them
down, so we have to let go of things that hinder us
from becoming wise.

By the way, *Double Eagle II* arrived safely and accomplished its mission.

*Father, help me to be willing to sacrifice whatever is necessary in
order to become wise.*

WISDOM & COMPASSION

Brethren, join in following my example, and note
those who so walk, as you have us for a pattern.
—PHIL. 3:17

One weekend, three young men decided to take a bicycle ride into the countryside. In spite of their inexperience, they covered forty miles in three and a half hours and patted each other on the back on their good time. "Not bad for the first time out," they told each other.

The next morning, as they prepared to head back home, they were met by a good friend, who had just cycled the forty-mile trip that morning and was ready to head back. An excellent cyclist, he paced the young cyclists back to town, and they made the return trip in just two and a half hours.

In the same way, we need the "pacing" of older believers who have more experience and knowledge in the Christian life. As we take our first "rides" in Christ, we can benefit from their background and progress as far as we can and as quickly as we can.

Why not find an older, more experienced Christian and ask if you can learn from him? You'll travel farther and faster than you would otherwise.

Father, help me to learn from those who have walked with you longer than I have.

He who disdains instruction despises his own soul,
but he who heeds reproof gets understanding.
—PROV. 15:32

Don, I don't believe it. You turned the report in two days early," said Sandy. "It was incredible that not only did you get it done early, but your analysis was right on. How did you do it? I'm really proud of you. You are living up to everything they said about you."

"Well," explained Don, "my dad taught me the value of working hard. He used to insist that I do my homework right when I got home from school, before I could go out and play. Over time, I developed the habit of using concentrated attention to get things done early and accurately."

Loose wires give out no musical notes, but when their ends are fastened, the piano, harp, or violin is born. Free steam drives no machine, but harnessed and confined with piston and turbine, it makes possible the great world of machinery. An unhampered river drives no dynamos, but dam it up and you can generate sufficient power to light a great city. In the same way, our lives must be disciplined if we are to be of any real service in the world.

Lord, help me to discipline my time and energy in order to accomplish what you desire.

WISDOM & COMPASSION

And everyone who competes for the prize is
temperate in all things. Now they do it to obtain a
perishable crown, but we for an imperishable
crown.
—1 COR. 9:25

In 1915, Lord Joseph Duveen, American head of the Duveen art firm, planned to send one of his experts to England to examine ancient pottery. He booked passage on the *Lusitania*. After the German warning that the liner might be torpedoed, he had second thoughts.

"Don't worry," his employee said. "I'm a strong swimmer, and when I read what was happening in the Atlantic, I began hardening myself by spending time in a tub of ice water each day. At first, I could only endure a few minutes, but this morning, I stayed in that tub two hours."

The man sailed, and the *Lusitania* was torpedoed. The young man was rescued after nearly five hours in the chilly ocean, still in excellent condition.

In the same way, we should demonstrate a heart of wisdom. Through the practice of devotional discipline, behavioral discipline, and discipline in doing good, we can condition ourselves for the battle ahead.

Father, help me to discipline myself in order to become a more godly person.

He who answers a matter before he hears it, it is
folly and shame to him.
                                            —PROV. 18:13

Back in the days of the Wild West, the story is told of a new commander who was sent to an army fort on the American frontier. Upon arriving, he set up conferences with both his army officers and the Indian chiefs. In one conference, he sat down with a leading chief and, working through a translator, he nervously asked the chief a number of questions. However, he received no reply and was astounded. After the meeting, he asked the translator why he had not gotten answers to his questions and if he had offended the chief. The translator replied, "That's what we call Indian time. The chief has enough respect for your questions to go away and think about them before answering them."

Too often we are guilty of framing an answer or rebuttal before the speaker ever finishes his sentence. Perhaps we would be wiser if we could develop the habit of listening intently.

Father, help me to listen and think through a matter before replying.

For what will it profit a man if he gains the whole world, and loses his own soul? —MARK 8:36

In 1978, there was a woman who needlessly lost her life during a flood in the hill country of Texas. As her daughter later explained to reporters, "My mother did not climb the tree with us. She lost her way before we got to the tree. See, she always kept every little bill and slip and stuff. She would not let go of her purse with those papers in it."

It was revealed later that the family was trying to make a human chain, holding hands to get through the raging torrent of water. But the mother had her insurance papers all gathered up in her hands and wouldn't drop those documents. Thus she was washed away.

Father, help me to make wise choices in establishing my priorities. Help me to know which things to hold on to and which to let go of.

A wise man will hear and increase learning, a man of understanding will attain wise counsel.
—PROV. 1:5

One night, a mother fixed a special meal for her family: turkey with mashed potatoes and gravy, corn, green beans, cranberry sauce, and pumpkin pie for dessert. It was the family's favorite meal, even more so because it came at a time other than Thanksgiving Day. While the aroma filled the house, the family filed in from their activities one by one and sat down at the table.

The youngest child, who had appeared only a few minutes before dinner, sat through the entire meal without eating. When asked why, he confessed that he had filled up on peanut butter at his friend's house. In settling for something average, he had lost his appetite for the best.

In the same way, we often lose our appetite for spiritual things because we have allowed ourselves to become filled up with lesser things.

Lord, help me to make wise choices in the things that I fill up my life with.

For we do not wrestle against flesh and blood,
but . . . against spiritual hosts of wickedness in the
heavenly places.
                                        —EPH. 6:12

Many years ago, a mental hospital devised a unique test to determine if their patients were ready to go back into the world. When someone was ready to be released, they would bring him into a room where a water faucet was left on so that the water overflowed from the sink onto the floor. The person was then handed a mop and a bucket and told to mop up the water. If the patient had enough sense to turn off the faucet before mopping up the water, he was ready to be released. But if the patient started mopping up the water while it was still flowing, he was kept for more treatment.

As Christians, we are confronted by evil in the world in which we live and the need to do battle with it. But, like the patients in the mental hospital, until we realize where the source of that evil is, we will be merely mopping up the water and will accomplish nothing.

Father, grant me wisdom in dealing with the evil around me.

A little sleep, a little slumber, a little folding of the hands to sleep—so shall your poverty come on you like a robber . . .
—PROV. 6:10–11

In the movie *Papillon,* the main character is a criminal who is imprisoned for life for crimes against the French state. The story follows his many attempts to escape from Devil's Island. The movie portrays the dreams he has while he is in prison. In one dream toward the end of the movie, he stands before a tribunal for a crime. He begs for mercy and pleads that he is not guilty of the crime for which he is being tried. The judge replies that he is not being tried for that particular crime, but rather for a crime that is the most heinous crime of the human race. Papillon asks what crime that is. The judge replies, "The crime of a wasted life." As he weeps bitterly, Papillon mutters the words, "Guilty, guilty." Sadly, the judge pronounces the sentence of death.

Father, help me to invest my life wisely in serving others rather than waste it on pleasing myself.

WISDOM & COMPASSION

*A wise man will hear and increase learning, and a
man of understanding will attain wise counsel.*
—PROV. 1:5

In August 1978, the first successful transatlantic balloon flight achieved success when *Double Eagle II* touched ground in a barley field outside the small village of Miserey, France. However, success did not come easy. Between 1873 and 1978, thirteen attempts had been made, with each one achieving the same result—failure. *Double Eagle* also failed in 1977 when it ended up in Iceland. But *Double Eagle II* was successful in making that historic six-day journey from Presque Isle, Maine, to Miserey, France.

What was the difference? What made one trip unsuccessful and the next a smashing success. Maxie Anderson, one of the crew, explained it this way, "I don't think that you can fly the Atlantic without experience, and that's one reason it hadn't been flown before. Success in any venture is just the intelligent application of failure."

Father, help me to gain wisdom by learning from my mistakes.

*I have heard of you, that the Spirit of God is in you,
and that light and understanding and excellent
wisdom are found in you.*
                                    —DAN. 5:14

John had a well-earned reputation as a wise man.
Granted, he had studied hard and long, and took many
years to build his business as a communications consultant. But if you asked his customers and his competi-
tors, they would say that his strength was his ability
to cut through all the smokescreens and identify the
company's root problems. Situations that took most
consultants weeks to work through and identify would
be solved by him in a matter of a few interviews.

Though his reputation for wisdom was well-
deserved, he was quick to say that it was a gift from
God. Each day, he would rise early to study the Scriptures and to pray. He would regularly spend time lay-
ing out the concerns and questions facing him, praying
that God would grant him wisdom and insight.

*Father, fill me with your Spirit and grant me wisdom and insight for
the problems I face today.*

*And this I pray, that your love may abound
still more and more in knowledge and all
discernment.*
                                          —PHIL. 1:9

Don was one of the most loving and caring people
Carl had ever met. But it seemed to him that some of
Don's efforts at care were misguided, or at least fell
short of accomplishing everything they could. When
attempting to help move a single parent into a new
home, he ignored the advice of two long-time friends
of the parent and went ahead with what he thought
best. While he helped him immediately, he actually
took him out of a situation that would have stretched
him and helped him grow. He had unwittingly aided
him in bailing out of trouble, a pattern very strong in
this person's life. As a result, he removed him from a
chance to learn perseverance.

Carl began to pray that God would grant Don a balance of love and wisdom. It was evident he had compassion in abundance. But he needed to channel it in
ways that were purposeful and helpful. His good inten-
tions and will needed guidance.

*Lord, help me to care for people in ways that will help their real,
deep needs.*

*I have more understanding than all my teachers,
for Your testimonies are my meditation.*

—PS. 119:99

Jason was a production manager for a printing firm. After completing high school, he had gotten into some trouble and landed in prison. After being released, he was introduced to Jesus Christ and committed his life to him. For ten years, he had risen at 4:30 every morning to study the Scriptures and to pray. It was not uncommon for him to spend two hours in personal devotions before going to work each day. A voracious reader, he read every book on theology and ministry that he could get his hands on.

Whenever anyone in the company had a personal problem, they would call Jason for advice. His opinion was widely respected throughout the organization. The executive officers would even invite him into their staff meetings to ask his advice on business decisions.

When someone asked him how he learned so much, he was quick to say that while he lacked a formal education, his knowledge and understanding came from his time in God's Word. It was there that he discovered the source of true wisdom.

Father, help me to study your word and gain wisdom from it.

*But when He saw the multitudes, He was moved
with compassion for them, because they were
weary and scattered, like sheep having no
shepherd.*

—MATT. 9:36

One evening, William Booth could not sleep, so he
went for a walk. For some reason, he walked down to
the poor side of London, and there, in the cover of
darkness, saw the impoverished and beaten half-lives
that existed in that setting. In the midst of the rain
beating down, he saw some of London's derelicts sleeping near the curbsides.

Returning home, his wife asked where he'd been.
"I've been to hell," was his reply.

Out of that nightmarish experience came the dream
of the Salvation Army. Had Booth not left the warmth
and security of his own home, he might never have
become aware of the needs of the homeless masses.

*Father, help me to risk stepping out of my comfort zone in order to
see and feel the needs of those around me.*

And when Jesus went out He saw a great multitude; and He was moved with compassion for them, and healed their sick. —MATT. 14:14

James was one of the most caring of men. He had spent his life as a special education teacher, and later, as a principal of a school for handicapped children. Now in his seventies and "retired," he was still as active as ever: organizing conferences, meeting with concerned parents, testifying before the school board, serving as a consultant for various school districts, and lobbying the state legislature for the handicapped. He remained a tireless advocate for the needs of the less fortunate.

When a family with two Down's Syndrome children started attending the church, he formed the Seekers—a Sunday school class—just for them. In addition to the class, he also organized a dinner and gym night twice a month on Friday nights. While the kids enjoyed games in the gym, he led a support group for their parents and ministered to their needs. He and his wife would also occasionally babysit for the parents so they could have a night out.

Father, when I see people with special needs, help me follow James's example and demonstrate compassion for them.

Whoever hides hatred has lying lips, and whoever spreads slander is a fool. —PROV. 10:18

Hey, Jonathan, did you hear about Peter?" asked Tim softly. "I saw he was called into the president's office earlier today. I bet he got fired. You know, he's been under a lot of pressure lately. And his work has really not been up to his usual standards. I can't see how the company can afford to keep carrying him when he's not pulling his own weight. I feel sorry for his wife and kids, but I can't see the president had any other choice. What do you think?"

Just then, Peter, who had overheard their conversation, rounded the corner. "What did you say, Tim? Do you want to know why Mr. Jameson had me in his office? He gave me a raise and a promotion to vice-president in charge of engineering. He said he appreciated how I performed under the recent pressure and deadlines and said he couldn't be more pleased with my work. Next time you start a rumor, at least get your facts straight."

Lord, help me not to jump to conclusions and spread lies about another person.

To do evil is like sport to a fool, but a man of understanding has wisdom. —PROV. 10:23

Bill, let's take a long lunch today," encouraged Allen. "I'm sure it's OK with the boss and we'll talk about the business deal most of the time. Besides, I bet he does it all the time anyway."

Allen had developed the reputation in the office for rarely putting in a full day's work. He routinely came in late, left early, and took extended lunch hours. During the rest of the day, you could either find him in the break room, or hanging around the copy machine talking to people. He was always taking extra office supplies home under the guise of working overtime at his house, though the supplies never found their way back to the office.

"Allen," interjected Bill, "I'd feel a lot better if we checked with him first. I want his input on this project as well. Why don't we invite him to join us? With his years of experience with the firm, we could learn a great deal from him."

Father, may my reputation be of one who is dependable and seeks the wisdom and advice of others.

The heart of him who has understanding seeks knowledge, but the mouth of fools feeds on foolishness.
                                        —PROV. 15:14

Mrs. Adams," said Alexander respectfully, "you've been a principal at this school for a long time. Could you give me some advice on how to become a better teacher? This is only my second year, and I feel like I have so much to learn. I feel like I understand my subject; but how to teach with more style; how to manage the classroom and the students better; well, I'm afraid I'm not very competent in those areas."

Alexander had a master's degree in chemistry and had elected to teach high school science. He had enjoyed school so much growing up that he wanted other students to have the same joy and love for learning that he did. He had survived his first year and was voted the outstanding teacher by the graduating seniors. But this was not enough.

He still wanted to learn more and become a skilled, master teacher. He took every opportunity he could to ask others for advice: important lessons they had learned, and anything they could suggest to do, or to read, in order to grow and improve his craft as a teacher.

Father, give me a desire to learn from others and improve in my knowledge and skills.

"The fear of the LORD is the beginning of wisdom."
—PROV. 9:10

Three-year-old Jonathan was watching his father play with a very large machine on the front lawn. He attached some kind of a bag to the back of the contraption and then poured what looked like water out of a red can into the top of the machine. His daddy then stepped on the thing, grabbed a handle with a rope tied to it and then pulled as hard as he could. The machine came roaring to life and Jonathan cried. He had just been introduced to the lawn mower and it scared him.

Whenever his dad took out the big red machine to mow the lawn, Jonathan made sure he kept a safe distance. He watched and observed how it cut the grass and sent it to the bag in back. When the bag became full, his dad would empty the bag into a trash can. He was amazed at what the mower did to leaves and sticks and tall grass—they disappeared and came out the back as small pieces!

Jonathan's fear led to a healthy respect, which led to a desire to observe and learn more. In the same way, our fear of God should lead to a desire to learn and know him better.

Lord, may my fear of you motivate me to know you better.

WISDOM & COMPASSION

Brethren, if a man is overtaken in any trespass, you who are spiritual restore such a one in a spirit of gentleness, considering yourself lest you also be tempted. Bear one another's burdens, and so fulfil the law of Christ.

—GAL. 6:1–2

Having recently admitted to having an affair, Ted, while truly repentant, was unsure of how the church leaders would respond and whether or not they would allow him to return to the fellowship. Quite honestly, he was afraid to meet Tom and Bill, his pastor and the chairman of the board. What would they say and do?

Ted's fears were put at ease when Bill began the conversation. "Ted, how old are you?" Bill gently asked. "Fifty-three," Ted replied. "Well," continued Bill, "I'm seventy-two, and I'm still tempted."

When we encounter another believer who has fallen into sin, rather than heap mounds of guilt, we need to lift them up. Rather than piously look down our nose at them, we need to remind ourselves that but for the grace of God, it could be us on the other side of the table. We need to lovingly and gently restore them to fellowship with God.

Father, allow me to gently bind and heal the wounds of my comrades who have fallen.

JUNE

Dealing with Emotions

*Be anxious for nothing, but in everything by prayer
and supplication, with thanksgiving, let
your requests be made known to God.*—PHIL. 4:6

What am I going to do?" Paul asked aloud for the umpteenth time. "How will we pay our bills if I get laid off from work? I don't have any other skills. Where would I go? I don't know anything else."

Two weeks ago, the rumor of an impending layoff had begun circulating through the company grapevine. The company was about to lose a contract, so the story went. When that happened, one-third of all employees would be laid off immediately.

Paul was certain that his name would be on that list. He was eating antacids like candy because his stomach was a churning mass of emotion. His ulcer was bound to land him in the hospital on this one, he told himself. For him, the job was not complete until it was worried over. And he was a master craftsman at worry.

He had to constantly remind himself that God could and would take care of him and his family. But he struggled with leaving it in his hands. Was he really big enough to handle this one? I don't know, he told himself.

Father, help me to trust you with my family's future rather than worry about the things I cannot control.

And not only that, but we also glory in tribulations,
knowing that tribulation produces perseverance;
and perseverance, character; and character, hope.
—ROM. 5:3–4

There is a strain of bamboo in Malaysia that requires great patience and perseverance to grow. The first year, you plant the seed, water and fertilize it, and nothing happens. The second year, you water and fertilize it, and nothing happens. The third year, you water and fertilize it, and nothing happens. The fourth year, you water and fertilize it, and nothing happens. But in the fifth year, you water and fertilize it, and it grows ninety feet in thirty days.

As fathers, there are many times we grow impatient and weary with the lack of progress and development we see in our kids. We want to throw in the towel and give up. They're never going to change! But like the bamboo farmer, we need to be committed to the long haul since results may not be seen until several years down the road. If we bail out early, we'll miss out on some explosive growth and changes.

Father, help me to be committed to the long-term growth and character development of my family.

For I am jealous for you with godly jealousy.
—2 COR. 11:2

In the midst of playing baseball in the backyard, Jim's six-year-old son's best friend, and next door neighbor, came out of his house. "Dad, can I go play with Brad?" he asked. "But son, we're playing baseball. Don't you want to play with me?" Jim asked, not really wanting to hear the answer he knew was coming. "Nah, I'd rather play with Brad," his son replied, all too honestly. Jim had a rival for his son's affection, and he was a six-year-old.

As he struggled with that thought, knowing that he'd better get a handle on it because it was only going to escalate, he suddenly was reminded that God felt the same way about him. He jealously desires our affection and attention as well. It breaks his heart when we show more interest in cars, sports, newspapers, television, yard work, hobbies, books, and family activities than we do in reading his word and prayer. It saddens him when we are more committed to serving ourselves and pursuing our own interests than we are in serving him.

If God were to examine your heart today, what rivals for his attention would he find? ─────────

Father, help me to be single minded in my devotion to you.

But godliness with contentment is great gain. . . .
And having food and clothing, with these we shall
be content.
                                            —1 TIM. 6:6, 8

The story is told of Charles Haddon Spurgeon, who was once given the tour of a vast mansion. His host showed him through room after room, commenting on the richly appointed furnishings, marble floors, and gold-leafed columns. As they left the home, his host asked Spurgeon how he liked the house. Spurgeon replied, "These are the things that make dying hard."

In the 90s, it is easy to get caught up with the greed and materialism so prevalent in our society. Buy this! You're worth it. . . . Don't leave home without it. . . . You deserve this fine, luxury automobile. . . . Buy a bigger home to impress your boss. . . . Wear the latest fashions. . . .

When we survey our garages, wardrobes, storage closets, home entertainment centers, houses, and bank accounts, we have to conclude like Spurgeon, "These are the things that make dying hard." Or are they?

The secret of contentment is not found in gaining more, but in learning to live with less. Add not to your possessions, but subtract from your desires.

Father, help me to learn to be content with less.

DEALING WITH EMOTIONS

An angry man stirs up strife, and a furious man
abounds in transgression. —PROV. 29:22

A boy once asked his father, "Dad, how do wars begin?"

"Well, take World War I," said the father. "That got started when Germany invaded Belgium."

Immediately his wife interrupted him. "Tell the boy the truth. It began because somebody was murdered." The husband drew himself up with an air of superiority and snapped back, "Who's answering this question, you or I?" Turning her back upon him in a huff, the wife stomped out of the room and slammed the door as hard as she could.

When the dishes stopped rattling in the cupboard, an uneasy silence followed, broken at length by the son when he said, "Daddy, you don't have to tell me anymore; I know now!"

Perhaps if we weren't so concerned about defending our own pride or position, we would be angry less often.

Father, rather than give full vent to my anger, help me to learn to control it.

DEALING WITH EMOTIONS

Let your conduct be without covetousness, and be content with such things as you have. . . .
—HEB. 13:5

An elderly Quaker set out to teach his neighbors a lesson one day. He placed a sign on a vacant piece of property he owned that read, "I will give this lot to anyone who is really satisfied."

A wealthy farmer read it as he rode by and said to himself, "Since my Quaker friend is going to give this piece of land away, I might as well have it as anyone else. I am rich and have all I need, so I am well able to qualify." So he rode up to the Quaker's door and, when the aged gentleman appeared, the farmer made his request.

The owner of the lot asked, "And art thou really satisfied?"

"I certainly am," the man replied. "I have all I need, and I am well satisfied."

"Friend," said the Quaker, "if thou art satisfied, then what dost thou want with my lot?"

As the Quaker intended, the question revealed the covetousness and discontent that was hidden in the man's heart.

Father, help me to be content with what you have given me.

DEALING WITH EMOTIONS

A sound heart is life to the body, but envy is rottenness to the bones.
                              —PROV. 14:30

There is a fable that Satan's agents were failing in their attempts to draw into sin a holy man who lived as a hermit in the desert of northern Africa. Since each attempt was met with failure, Satan, furious at the incompetence of his lieutenants, decided to get personally involved. He explained, "The reason you have failed is that your methods are too crude for one such as this. Watch as I show you what to do."

Approaching the holy man with great care, he whispered softly in his ear, "Your brother has just been made Bishop of Alexandria." Instantly a great scowl formed over the man's mouth and his eyes tightened up. Satan had been successful.

Turning to his henchmen, Satan said, "Envy is often our best weapon against those who seek holiness."

Father, protect me from envying others.

From whom the whole body, . . . causes growth of
the body for the edifying of itself in love.
—EPH. 4:16

Sir Michael Costa was conducting an orchestra rehearsal. Halfway through the session, with the trumpets blaring, drums rolling, and violins singing their
rich melody, the piccolo player began to feel sorry for
himself and think: "What good am I doing? No one
ever listens to me. I never have a solo. I may as well
quit playing. I bet nobody can hear me anyway." And
with that, he placed his instrument to his lips, but
made no sound. Within moments the conductor cried,
"Stop! Stop! Where's the piccolo?"

Most of the people did not know the piccolo was
missing, but the most important one did.

There are times in the Christian life where we feel
insignificant, and start feeling sorry for ourselves. We
downplay our gifts and abilities, and conclude that we
do not make a difference. We need to remind ourselves
that God knows when we do not play the part assigned
to us, even if others do not.

Father, thank you that you listen intently to the part that I play.

DEALING WITH EMOTIONS

I will praise You, for I am fearfully and wonderfully made.
                                        —PS. 139:14

The story is told of a girl who was the daughter of one of the royal families of Europe, but had a rather large nose that, in her eyes, destroyed her beauty and left her seeing herself as ugly. Her family hired the services of one of the finest plastic surgeons to change the contour of her nose. Having done his work, he removed the bandages and stepped back to admire his work. It was a total success. All the ugly contours were gone and what remained was beautiful. When the incisions healed and the redness disappeared, she would indeed be a gorgeous girl. He held up a mirror for the girl to see, but when she saw her reflection, she blurted out, "Oh, I knew it wouldn't work." So deeply imbedded was the image of herself that when she saw her reflection, she couldn't see any change.

It took six months for the girl to accept the fact that she was an attractive person, and it wasn't until this point that her behavior began to change accordingly.

In order for my self-image to change, I must learn to see myself as God sees me, fearfully and wonderfully made.

Father, allow me to view myself through your eyes and help me to accept myself.

"Judge not, that you be not judged."
—MATT. 7:1

A lady in an airport was waiting for her cross-country flight. To pass the time, she bought a book to read and a package of cookies to eat. After taking her seat in the terminal and becoming engrossed in her book, she noticed that the man one seat away was fumbling to open the package of cookies on the seat between them. She was so shocked that a stranger would eat her cookies that she really didn't know what to say, so she just reached over and took one of the cookies and ate it. The man didn't say anything, but soon reached over and took another. Well, she wasn't going to let him eat all of them, so she also grabbed another. When they were down to one cookie, the man broke it in half, took one half, left the other half, and got up and left. The woman couldn't believe the man's nerve, but soon the announcement for her own flight sounded and she boarded her plane.

Once aboard, but still angry at the man's audacity, she reached into her purse for a tissue. To her surprise, there lay her still-unopened package of cookies. To her chagrin, she learned not to judge others too harshly.

Father, before I am critical of others, help me to examine my own heart.

*Do not boast about tomorrow, for you do not know
what a day may bring forth.* —PROV. 27:1

Placed next to the bar in the club house of a golf course was a sign that read, "Free beer tomorrow." People would read the sign and return the next day expecting to receive free beer. When they did, they discovered the sign read, "Free beer *tomorrow*."

The fantasy of tomorrow stunts growth. The belief that "when things get better tomorrow" can put our train on to a side track where we sit and watch as life passes us by. It creates dangerous fantasies: if I'm going to win the lottery tomorrow, I don't need to learn to budget today. If a marriage conference is going to solve all my marital woes, then I don't have to learn to communicate better today. If I wait for my circumstances to change, then I don't have to work on changing my character. If I wait for the change to take place out there, then I don't have to make any changes in here . . .

When things get better tomorrow . . . a dangerous fantasy indeed.

Father, help me to face today and to make the changes that I need to.

For you have need of endurance, so that after you have done the will of God, you may receive the promise.
—HEB. 10:36

Whenever we are tempted to give up and quit because we don't see immediate results, it is good to be reminded of the discovery of the planet Pluto by young Clyde Tombaugh.

Astronomers had already calculated a probable orbit for this "suspected" heavenly body, though it had never been seen. Tombaugh began his search in March of 1929. Poring over scores of telescopic photographs, each showing tens of thousands of star images, he would examine them under the blink comparator, or dual microscope. Sometimes it would take three days to examine one photograph. As Tombaugh described it himself, the work was "brutal, tedious, exhausting, eye-cracking work." Month by month, star by star, he examined twenty million images. Finally, on February 18, 1930, as he was blinking a pair of photographs in the constellation Gemini he suddenly came upon the image of Pluto. And the most dramatic astronomic discovery in nearly one hundred years was made possible by patience.

Father, help me to be patient and to persevere in completing the task you have for me.

*You will keep him in perfect peace, whose mind is
stayed on You, because he trusts in You.*

—ISA. 26:3

There is a painting titled "Peace." It looks to be anything but that as it depicts waves crashing against the
jagged rocks. With blackened clouds overhead and
dashing rain, it portrays the violence of a crushing
storm. How could anyone call this peace?

Yet, down in a small corner of the painting, tucked
away in the rocks, is a little bird sitting on her nest.
She is totally oblivious to the storm raging all about
her.

Many times we feel as if we are caught in the midst
of a storm. Job layoffs, illnesses, the death of a loved
one, pressure at work, home, school, breakdown in
family communication, broken promises, and other
disappointments crash down around us.

In the midst of all of these various pressures and
stresses, we can experience peace as we trust in God.

Father, help me to give you my cares and to rest in you today.

DEALING WITH EMOTIONS

*And the peace of God, which surpasses all
understanding, will guard your hearts and
minds through Christ Jesus.*

—PHIL. 4:7

Eric Barker, a missionary from Great Britain, spent over fifty years in Portugal preaching the gospel, much of it under adverse circumstances. During World War II, the situation became so critical that he listened to advice and sent his wife and eight children home to England for safety. In addition, his sister and her three children were also evacuated while Barker remained behind to conclude some business for the mission.

The Sunday after his family left, Barker stood before the congregation and said, "I've just received word that all my family have arrived safely home." It was only later that the meaning of his words were known to his parish. Prior to the meeting, he had been given a message that a submarine had torpedoed the ship, and everyone on board had drowned. Since all were believers, Barker knew they were in heaven.

In spite of his overwhelming grief, this firm conviction enabled Eric to live above his circumstances. And the peace of God will allow us to do the same.

Lord, grant me peace in the midst of a situation that I don't understand.

DEALING WITH EMOTIONS

*But you are a chosen generation, a royal
priesthood, a holy nation, His own special
people, . . .*
　　　　　　　　　　　　　　　　—1 PETER 2:9

G. Campbell Morgan, great preacher of another generation, experienced rejection early in his ministry. He was one of 150 young men who applied for entrance into the Wesleyan ministry in 1888. While he had passed his written exam, he still faced the daunting task of giving a trial sermon in front of a panel. When the results were released, Morgan's name was among the 105 who were rejected.

He wired his father with one word: "Rejected." He then wrote in his diary: "Very dark. Everything seems still. He knoweth best." The reply to his wire arrived back quickly. It read, "Rejected on earth, accepted in heaven. Dad."

As G. Campbell Morgan went on to demonstrate, rejection on earth is often of little consequence. As his father wisely understood, rejection on earth is of no consequence in heaven.

Lord, when I feel rejected, remind me that you have accepted me.

. . . and in the time of their trouble, when they cried to You, You heard from heaven; and . . . saved them from the hands of their enemies.

—NEH. 9:27

Many years ago, a tall sailing ship was caught in a terrible storm and was lost at sea in a deserted area. Only one crewman survived, washed ashore on a small uninhabited island. Each day he looked for passing ships and prayed desperately that God would send help and deliverance. Eventually, he managed to build a small hut and store what little he had recovered from the wreck along with those things he had made on the island.

One day, after returning from his search for food, the sailor was appalled to see a column of smoke. He discovered that his hut was in flames and everything he needed for survival was destroyed. Stunned and overcome with grief and despair, he spent a sleepless night trying to figure out what to do next.

The next morning, to his amazement, a ship was anchored off shore and a boat was rowing toward him. After meeting the captain, he learned that they had seen his smoke signal the day before, but had been prevented by the tide from arriving sooner.

Even in the midst of despair, God can bring a blessing out of what seems to be a curse.

Father, help me to look to you in the midst of despair.

DEALING WITH EMOTIONS

Therefore we do not lose heart. Even though our outward man is perishing, yet the inward man is being renewed day by day.   —2 COR. 4:16

Some flowers, such as the rose, must be crushed in order for their full fragrance to be released. Fruits such as the sycamore must be bruised if they are to attain ripeness and sweetness. Metals such as gold must pass through the refiner's fire if they are to become pure.

In the same way, the attaining of godliness—the process of becoming a mature Christian—requires similar special handling. Spiritual discipline and maturity cannot be gained without pain, suffering, trouble, adversity, trials, and even temptation.

When we encounter and pass through difficult circumstances, we can be strengthened and renewed by the knowledge of the end result. While the process may not be enjoyable, it will allow us to grow to be more like Jesus. That knowledge and assurance encourages perseverance.

Father, help me not to give up when I am tried and tested.

But when he saw that the wind was boisterous, he was afraid; and beginning to sink he cried out, saying, "Lord, save me!"
—MATT. 14:30

He felt like he was going down for the last time. The undercurrents of work, family, school, and other responsibilities were pulling him under. The "only one month of overtime" had stretched into four. He was consistently working 60 hours a week with no relief in sight. His hectic and demanding schedule left him with little energy to give to his wife and kids. Missing his son's last little league game didn't ease his guilt, either. In addition, the responsibility of caring for his aging mother weighed on him. And on top of all of that, he was supposed to keep up with the course work for his MBA. "Why had he started that stupid program anyway?" he berated himself again.

As the riptide of despair grabbed at his senses, he cried out, "God, help me! I cannot carry all this by myself. I confess I've tried to be too independent. Please rescue me. I need help." _____

Lord, before I start drowning, help me to reach out to you for help.

Jesus wept.
—JOHN 11:35

Big boys don't cry." "Buck up and be a man." "It's not manly to show your emotions." "C'mon, show some backbone. What's the matter? Are you some kind of a sissy?"

As John sat through his father's funeral, these thoughts and others like them ran through his mind. While he maintained a dispassionate stoicism on the outside, his emotions were a churning, bubbling cauldron inside. He kept telling himself, "You've got to be strong for Mom. The girls need you to carry them through this." He could not break down, not now at least.

Society maintains the illusion that men do not feel or show emotion. Our heroes have "ice water in their veins" or are "cool under pressure."

We are light years removed from Jesus, who was deeply moved, troubled, and burst into tears at the death of a friend. He was agitated, and his grief was spontaneous. Secure in who he was, he was not afraid to demonstrate his concern and emotion.

Father, help me to show others how I feel, especially when I am hurting.

Casting all your care upon Him, for He cares for you.
—1 PETER 5:7

Son," said Dr. Jones, "you've got to find a way to deal with your worry. Your body is just not designed to handle this. This is the third time in the last year we've put you in the hospital for a bleeding ulcer. Keep it up and you may not live through the next one.

"Let me make a suggestion. Here's what I do when I go home. Just outside my front door is a tree. In fact, I call it my 'Worrying Tree.' As I go by, I touch the branches and I mentally tell myself that I am hanging my worries on the tree. That way, when I go inside the house, I can enjoy my family without being nagged by my concerns. When I leave for the hospital the next morning, my worries are still on the tree waiting for me to pick them up. Sometimes it seems like they've multiplied overnight."

While a worry tree is an effective tool to hang our problems on, wouldn't it be much more effective to pile our worries on the One who cares deeply for us and offers peace in return?

Father, when I feel burdened and buried by problems, remind me to give them to you.

DEALING WITH EMOTIONS

> *"Which of you by worrying can add one cubit to
> his stature?"*
> —MATT. 6:27

A friend used to work for a structural steel detailer. His job was to follow the architectural drawings and detail the structural steel for high-rise builders. The owner of that firm had a favorite saying, "Just get the drawings done, even if they're not complete. The contractor will worry the beams into place anyway."

The picture of someone moving a structural steel beam into position by sheer worry is almost laughable. But then again, many people live by the philosophy that the job is not done until it's worried over. If there's nothing to worry about, then they're concerned that they might have forgotten something. "This is too easy," they say. "Something is bound to go wrong."

Worry's voracious appetite can consume thousands of hours in the course of one's lifetime. And for what? More often than not, it simply devours energy that could have been better spent on finding a lasting solution.

Lord, remind me of the futility of worry and that I should give my concerns to you.

> ". . . and lo, I am with you always, even to the end
> of the age."
> —MATT. 28:20

Jonathan hated crowds. It was not that he didn't like people. In fact, just the opposite was true. He craved being with people. He had a seemingly unquenchable thirst for conversation and meaningful relationships. The problem was that he was new in town and had not yet developed any close friendships.

Having just graduated from college with a degree in tax accounting, he had moved across the country to take a job with a Big Eight accounting firm. As an auditor, it seemed like he was always on the road. Consequently, this too hindered him in putting down roots and making friends.

Craving relationships and friendships, he would find the biggest party and invite himself in. But instead of feeling welcomed, he felt more isolated. The larger the crowd, the more it reminded him of how alone he really was. The only things that helped him keep his sanity were the pictures of his parents and friends in his wallet. Regardless of how lonely he felt, he knew they still loved him.

Father, when I feel lonely, remind me that you are always with me.

DEALING WITH EMOTIONS

*"You have heard . . . "You shall not murder," . . .
But I say to you that whoever is angry with his
brother without a cause shall be in danger of hell
fire.*

—MATT. 5:21-22

Coaching volleyball one evening, Sam turned his attention to the group working on their blocking skills at the net. In another part of the gym, a group was serving, and still another group was running other drills. Out of the corner of his eye, he saw Jim attempt a serve that went wildly out of control, striking Kevin, who was on a different court, in the back of the head. Kevin whirled and let loose with a string of expletives. "You clumsy oaf! Why don't you watch what you're doing? What a dumb jerk."

By strict definition, very few of us have actually murdered someone. But how many of us have ever run another through verbally? How many times have we crushed a coworker's self-image or cut his performance to shreds in front of him and others, or simply wished he were dead? When we parry with a verbal saber and our fingerprints are on a verbal smoking gun, we are just as guilty of murder in our hearts as if we held the actual, physical weapon.

Father, cleanse my heart of any hateful thoughts I have toward others.

JUNE 24

"You have heard . . . 'You shall not commit adultery.' But I say to you that whoever looks at a woman to lust for her has already committed adultery with her in his heart." —MATT. 5:27, 28

Man, did you see the new gal in the office?" asked Caleb. "Whew, what I wouldn't give to get her in a closet and . . . "

"Didn't you tell me you were happily married?" interrupted Mark before the conversation degenerated.

"Yeah, but just because you're on a diet doesn't mean you stop looking at the menu. If you know what I mean, huh, kid?"

While most men would adamantly say that they would never cheat on their wives, how many would be honest about admitting that they've mentally undressed another woman? How many would confess that they have contemplated the curves of a woman other than their wife and wondered how they would feel?

Men, let's not delude ourselves. Adultery is committed far more often in the mind than it ever is in bed. Protect your heart from lust.

God, help me to focus my thoughts and desires only on my wife.

DEALING WITH EMOTIONS

JUNE 25

*To everything there is a season, a time for every
purpose under heaven.*
—ECCL. 3:1

Plant and harvest. Build and settle. Marry and have
children. Buy and sell. Speak and listen. Work and
play. The seasons of life have a rhythm all their own.

Quite often, the reason we feel impatient is because
we are out of season. Like an instrumentalist that becomes confused and starts playing on the upbeat instead of the downbeat, we, too, become disoriented
when our rhythm is off. Rather than waiting, observing, and playing the part as it is written, we rush to
try to catch up.

In order to be more patient, we can profit greatly
by learning from a farmer. The hard work of planting
is followed by long months of growth and cultivation
before the harvest is ready. And even then, the field
must lie fallow for a time before planting again. We
cannot hurriedly rush the seed back into the ground.
We must learn and master the rhythm of the seasons.

*Father, help me to be a student of the seasons in order to learn
patience.*

Just as He chose us in Him before the foundation of the world, that we should be holy and without blame before Him in love.
—EPH. 1:4

We all desire relationships in which we are accepted, valued, and wanted. We desperately long for this esteem from our peers, but seldom experience the "real thing."

Countless stories are written about teenagers who accept life-threatening dares in the hopes of being accepted by their peers, or business people who compromise their integrity and ethics to join an elite, inner circle. We read of men and women who are driven to succeed because they believe the lie that says their value is determined by the quality and level of their performance. Or how about the teenager or lonely single who sacrifices his virginity for the chance to experience closeness and the feeling of being wanted.

For the Christian, none of this futile struggle is necessary because we have been chosen by God before time ever began. We belong, we matter, we have been accepted. No longer outcasts or second-class citizens, we are part of his family.

Lord, thank you for choosing me to be part of your family.

DEALING WITH EMOTIONS

*When He had made a whip of cords, He drove
them all out of the temple . . . and poured out the
changers' money and overturned the tables.*
—JOHN 2:15

Gentle Jesus, meek and mild.

Where did we ever develop the cardboard cutout of a wimpy, emotionless Jesus? Why can we easily picture Christ holding children on his lap, but we resist the image of him rolling up his sleeves and throwing furniture around the room? A Jesus who can bless and multiply the loaves and the fish is easy to comprehend, but one snapping a cat-o'-nine-tails stretches our imagination beyond its limits.

Contrary to popular opinion, it is possible to be angry and not sin. But to do so, we must follow the example of Jesus. It must be directed at sin, evil or injustice. It must be controlled anger and not merely heated passion. And there must be no hatred, malice, resentment, or selfishness involved.

Lord, help me to control and restrain my anger.

*Now one . . . returned, and with a loud voice
glorified God, and fell down on his face at His
feet, giving Him thanks. . . .* —LUKE 17:15, 16

The story is told of a six feet, seven inches offensive
tackle who had never complimented his wife on anything. Having recently become a Christian, he realized
how insensitive and ungrateful he had been for the
first ten years of their marriage—but he was terrified
to admit it and didn't know what to do.

Finally, one evening after picking at his dinner and
pushing his vegetables around the plate, he stood up,
walked over to his wife, pulled out her chair, grabbed
her in both hands, and blurted out, "Woman! That
meal was tremendous! Thanks." Overcome with fear
and emotion, she fainted.

Now while we laugh, how many of us act as if we
deserve our wives, service and aren't required to
make any comments unless it is of poor quality? How
many of us routinely compliment and thank our wives
for all their hard work? When was the last time you
said a simple thanks without being reminded?

Father, help me to compliment my wife and say "Thank you!"

*Therefore do not worry about tomorrow, for
tomorrow will worry about its own things.
Sufficient for the day is its own trouble.*
—MATT. 6:34

As the rumors of impending layoffs circulated through the company plant, tensions were raised and anxiety filled the air. "What am I going to do?" thought Art. "I've worked here for twenty years. I only have two more to go until retirement. Where will I go? How am I going to start a new career at my age?"

It seemed that every two years, rumors of another round of layoffs were started and spread, and each time Art survived—though he sweated bullets in the process. While he knew he shouldn't worry, he did it anyway. He was well aware that his doctor said it wasn't good for his heart and he knew the Bible said not to do it, as well. But, if the truth be known, he just liked to worry. While the circumstances may have been out of his control, he felt like he was at least doing something by worrying.

In the end, there were no layoffs. True to form, in spite of his worry, the company righted itself and kept on going. Once again he had worried for nothing.

Lord, help me not to worry about the things I have no control over.

*Make no friendship with an angry man, and with a
furious man do not go, lest you learn his ways and
set a snare for your soul.* —PROV. 22:24–25

I'm concerned about the friends you hang around
with, Jeffrey," said his mother. "Those boys seem like
they're up to no good. They're out of control and I'm
afraid you'll be just like them. Please tell me you won't
be friends with them."

Reluctantly, Jeffrey listened to his mother and
stopped associating with that group of boys. Only
years later did his mother's wisdom truly sink in.

He attended his twentieth high school reunion and
heard news of the boys "up to no good." One had died
in an automobile accident because of reckless driving,
two were in prison on drug trafficking charges, and
the other one hadn't been seen in fifteen years. It
dawned on him that he had gotten out just in time.
Fortunately for him, his mother had been a good judge
of character, after all.

Father, help me to guide my children in their choice of friends.

DEALING WITH EMOTIONS

JULY

Displaying Joy

Rejoice in the Lord always. Again I will say, rejoice!
—PHIL. 4:4

Lost: One sense of humor. Generally identified as a smiling face, a cheerful, friendly grin, or hearty laugh. Last seen as a twinkle in the eye or in the upturned corners of the mouth. If found, return to owner. Reward will be generous.

In interviews around the country, women were asked what they would most like to have in their home. You would expect them to say more and better communication, or to want husbands who open up and share their feelings. But they didn't. The overwhelming response was *laughter*. They want their families to smile more, enjoy each other's company, to have pleasant conversations at the dinner table—they want to laugh more often.

In the frantic pace of the 90s, we've lost our ability to laugh and smile. We need to put out an APB on our missing joy. We need to retrace our steps to discover where we left it. We need to experience outrageous joy again for the first time.

Lord, restore to me the joy of my salvation.

. . . singing and making melody in your heart to the Lord, giving thanks always for all things to God the Father in the name of our Lord Jesus Christ.
—EPH. 5:19–20

Wherever he went, you always found Sam with a smile on his face and humming a tune. It seemed like he was perpetually cheerful. His happy demeanor used to drive his coworkers crazy because they thought it was all a front. They finally understood the nature of his outlook when they saw how he responded to an airline cancellation.

He was flying on a business trip with two coworkers when their flight was canceled due to equipment failure. All around him, people were cursing and bemoaning their lack of luck. Sam's response was still one of cheer. "How can you act this way?" they badgered him. "Aren't you upset?"

"Well, I don't like the idea of staying overnight in a strange city any more than you do. But I've discovered that, while I don't have a choice about my flight arrangements, I do have a choice about how I respond. They can cancel my flight, but they cannot cancel my day. This may appear to be a big problem, but I still serve a God who is bigger than any problem I may have."

Father, remind me that you are in control of all of life so that I can respond to the problems I encounter with joy and thanksgiving.

DISPLAYING JOY

JULY 3

Finally, my brethren, rejoice in the Lord. For me to write the same things to you is not tedious, but for you it is safe.
—PHIL. 3:1

Sam and Ginny were driving on a long trip and stopped at a full-service gas station. After the station attendant had washed their car's windshield, Sam said to the station attendant, "It's still dirty. Wash it again."

So the station attendant complied. After washing it again, Sam angrily said, "It's still dirty. Don't you know anything about how to wash a windshield?"

Just then Ginny reached over, removed her husband's glasses from his face, cleaned them with a tissue, and handed them back to him. He then put them back on and behold—the windshield was clean!

One's mental attitude has a great deal to do with how we look at life. The whole world can appear pretty bleak if we have a depressed mental attitude. Yet how bright the world can appear if we have a joyful attitude of hope.

Father, help me to view life through a joyful heart.

DISPLAYING JOY

*All the days of the afflicted are evil, but he who is
of a merry heart has a continual feast.*
—PROV. 15:15

Norman Cousins has written a fascinating book on
the benefits of laughter entitled *The Anatomy of an
Illness from the Perspective of the Patient.* In it, he tells
the story of being diagnosed with a life-threatening illness. His collagen was breaking down. (Collagen is the
stuff that holds our cells together—he was literally
coming apart.)

Since there was no known cure for his condition, he
decided to take matters into his own hands. With his
doctor's permission, he started a treatment which included vitamins, healthy diet, and laugh therapy. He
checked out a variety of Laurel and Hardy and Marx
Brothers films as well as other comedians, and he
watched them several hours a day. He discovered that
ten minutes of solid laughter brought him two hours
of pain-free sleep.

With his unusual regimen, he laughed himself back
to health and discovered the connection between one's
emotional state and health.

Have you taken your laughter vitamin today?

Father, help me to laugh at myself today.

DISPLAYING JOY

See that no one renders evil for evil to anyone, but always pursue what is good both for yourselves and for all. —1 THESS. 5:15

Former President William McKinley was a man who understood that you can accomplish more by kindness than by force. During one of his presidential campaigns, a reporter continually misrepresented his views. During the campaign, the weather turned bitterly cold. Despite his lack of warm clothing, the reporter continued following McKinley.

On one particular evening, the president-to-be was riding in his closed carriage while the reporter was shivering on the driver's seat outside. McKinley stopped the carriage and invited the lad to put on his coat and ride inside with him. The reporter protested that McKinley knew that he was the opposition and that he wasn't going to stop opposing him during the campaign. McKinley knew that, but he was not out to seek revenge. In the remaining days of the campaign, the reporter continued to oppose McKinley, but never again did he write anything unfair or biased about the future president.

Father, help me to demonstrate kindness to those who oppose me.

DISPLAYING JOY

*Therefore comfort each other and edify one
another, just as you also are doing.*
—1 THESS. 5:11

During the season of Super Bowl I, the great quarterback of the Green Bay Packers, Bart Starr, had developed an incentive scheme with his oldest son regarding his schoolwork. For every perfect paper Bart Junior brought home from school, Starr gave him ten cents. That seemed to work well and motivated the young boy to work hard.

After a particularly rough football game against St. Louis, in which Starr felt he had performed poorly, he returned home late one night, weary and battered. There attached to his pillow was a note: "Dear Dad, I thought you played a great game. Love, Bart." Taped to the note were two dimes.

What better way to display joy than by using it to encourage and build up others.

Father, help to me say words of encouragement to my wife and children today.

DISPLAYING JOY

Fulfill my joy by being like-minded, having the
same love, being of one accord, of one mind.
—PHIL. 2:2

Bear Bryant, the legendary former head football coach at the University of Alabama, was once interviewed about his view on national recognition for his players. It had just been announced that only one player from his team that particular year had been named as an All-American. The interviewer asked Bryant if he was disappointed. He answered that, of course, he was. But he went on to add that because his goal was always team effort, either all of his team should be All-American or none should be. He did not want one player to stand out at the expense of the team.

A source of joy is found in developing and strengthening a sense of unity, whether it is in a family, a church, a business, or an organization. Working together for a common purpose not only enables us to accomplish more together than we can apart, but also brings with it a great sense of satisfaction.

Lord, allow me to be a catalyst for unity rather than a roadblock.

DISPLAYING JOY

*In everything give thanks; for this is the will of God
in Christ Jesus for you.*   —1 THESS. 5:18

The evergreen tree earns its name because it is always green despite the changes in weather around it. Whether in the midst of the sweltering heat of summer or the dead cold of winter, the tree stands "ever green."

In much the same way, our lives are to be characterized by an enduring thankfulness regardless of the changes in the season of life around us. We are to give thanks in the heat of a pressured week. When stung by the icy cold of pain and sadness, we are to rejoice.

This doesn't mean we necessarily like or enjoy the heat or the cold. But it does mean we can give thanks for what they will produce. In the midst of change, we can be thankful for a God who does not change himself and who controls and allows the changes.

Whether the seasons remain constant or constantly changing, we are to stand "ever green," always thankful.

Father, grant me the grace to be thankful today.

DISPLAYING JOY

*Always in every prayer of mine making request for
you all with joy.*
—PHIL. 1:4

Whenever Gene sat down to pray, images and faces
always flashed through his mind. He thought of his
parents and the day they introduced him to Jesus.
There, beside the bed in his room, they led him in
praying to receive Christ.

He thought of his youth pastor, John, who discipled,
encouraged, and challenged him to grow during high
school. He was reminded of Tony, who saw leadership
potential in him and gave him his first opportunity to
teach a Bible study.

He thought of the various people who were with
him in small groups over the years. Tony and Kay
trusted Christ in his living room. Joel wrestled with his
doubts as they flipped burgers on the grill in the back
yard. Phil shared his decision to attend seminary over
dinner in the kitchen.

The people he was closest to came as a result of the
gospel. Their memories brought him joy.

---

*Father, thanks for the people who have impacted my life because of
their commitment to you.*

Then our mouth was filled with laughter, and our tongue with singing. Then they said among the nations, "The LORD has done great things for them."

—PS. 126:2

It was the bottom of the ninth, with two outs, and the Dodgers were behind in the first game of the World Series. The Oakland Athletics ace reliever, Dennis Eckersly, was on the mound. The game, for all practical purposes, was over.

Los Angeles called on a pinch hitter, Kirk Gibson. Even though he was the team leader, he was relegated to the bench because he had torn up his knee. What was Tommy Lasorda thinking? Even if Gibson hit the ball, he couldn't run.

Working the count to his favor, Gibson teed-off on a two-strike fastball, hitting it out of the park. The Dodgers had come from behind to win the game! The stadium erupted with exaltation. Dodger fan living rooms became bedlam as people hugged and cheered.

In the same way that we cheer our sports heroes, we rejoice and cheer in the greatness of God and the demonstrations of his goodness in our lives.

God, help me to shout about your exploits and what you have done for me.

DISPLAYING JOY

And Sarah said, "God has made me laugh, so that all who hear will laugh with me." —GEN. 21:6

Remember the time at Aunt Sarah's wedding when the best man passed out and crashed into the ivy?"

"Yeah, but do you recall the look on Sarah's face when her new husband pushed the cake past her mouth and into her ear during the reception? It was hilarious!"

"Do you remember last year's fishing trip when you were loading the boat and had one foot on the dock and the other on the boat?"

"Yeah, and you untied the docking line and the boat started to drift away from the dock, leaving me to do the splits and fall into the lake."

"I almost died laughing on that one."

Reliving past joys and pleasant memories with good friends is one of God's gifts to us. Recalling times of gladness and the ability to laugh at ourselves later on doubles our sense of joy.

———————

Father, remind me of the good things you've done in my life.

*Even in laughter the heart may sorrow, and the end
of mirth may be grief.*
—PROV. 14:13

On a bus ride back from a high school camp, Angie, the class clown, bared her soul with the frustration that no one took her seriously. Since she was always smiling, no one realized that she was crying inside. With an alcoholic father, and three of her four siblings divorced or separated, peals of laughter merely covered up the hole in her heart. "Why doesn't anyone look deep enough to see my pain?" she sobbed.

Dennis was known for his quick wit, one-liners, and wry sense of humor. Most people thought he could be a stand-up comic if he wanted to. But as Dennis explained, his quick humor was a smokescreen, hiding a deep fear of rejection and a nervousness that threatened to paralyze him in front of people. "The only way to get through it is to make people laugh and take the focus off me," he explained.

Like a shiny movie set, pain can hide under the surface of pleasure.

Father, grant me the sensitivity to look behind the facade and feel the hurts underneath the humor.

DISPLAYING JOY

*And Hannah prayed . . . "My heart rejoices in the
LORD; . . . because I rejoice in Your salvation."*
—1 SAM. 2:1

Mark," exclaimed Jeremy over the phone, "you'll
never guess what happened. Remember how I asked
you to pray about my application for a scholarship to
graduate school? Because of a mix-up in dates and
scheduling, I applied late for the program. Two months
ago, I received a letter saying that they were planning
on giving out 2,500 scholarships and that I was 432 on
the waiting list. While some on the waiting list received
aid, they seldom got past the first 150. Three weeks
ago, I received another letter explaining that they
were up to 289, but not to get my hopes up since there
was a limited amount of money left. Today, I opened
my mail and there was a letter congratulating me for
receiving a full scholarship. When I register tomorrow
for the new semester, I can take a full load and I'm not
going to have to borrow any money at all. Isn't that
incredible? God is so good!"

*Lord, help me to rejoice with others in how you have delivered them
from difficulty.*

O Lord, I pray, please let Your ear be attentive
to . . . Your servants who desire to fear Your
name; . . .
                                          —NEH. 1:11

Sam, this may sound strange," offered Tim, "but I don't appreciate the way you just asked God to damn your car. His name is very special to me, and I don't like to hear it used as a curse."

"You've got to be kidding," exclaimed Sam with a string of expletives attached. "What planet did you just step off of? That attitude went out with the horse and buggy. Are you some kind of holier-than-thou religious freak?"

In this day and age, people who take pride and joy in revering the name of God are few and far between. Swearing, cussing, invoking God's name to curse something or someone, expletives deleted, exclamations of anger—these have become the rule rather than the exception. We've come a long way from the Hebrew scribes who would not even write the name of Yahweh or Jehovah without washing their hands, using a new pen, and even then, writing "Lord" as a substitute. God's name was too holy to even be written, let alone dragged through the mud as a curse. We've come a long way, but it may not exactly be progress.

Father, help me to treat your name with the respect it deserves.

DISPLAYING JOY

But his delight is in the law of the LORD, and in His law he meditates day and night. —PS. 1:2

Paul, I need some advice about my relationship with my boss. I really have a hard time respecting him," said Terry.

"Well, you know what the Bible says about that, don't you?" interjected Paul.

After discussing the situation for some time, Terry asked, "Paul, how'd you get to be so wise?"

"Well, I don't have a lot of formal education and I never went to college. But after I became a Christian at the age of thirty, I decided to find out how God wanted me to live. For the last ten years, I've gotten up at 5:00 A.M. every day to read and study God's Word. When I first started, it was really hard and I resisted the alarm clock. But now, I'd have to say that it's the best part of my day. No bragging intended, but I don't think I've missed a day in the last five or six years. When I'm hurried and I miss that time, it changes my whole outlook and the way I approach the day. I can honestly say that I love reading and thinking about what God has said through the Bible."

Father, help me to demonstrate how much I value your Word by how I arrange my schedule to study it.

DISPLAYING JOY

*And my soul shall be joyful in the LORD; it shall
rejoice in His salvation.*
                                    —PS. 35:9

Do you ever reflect on the meaning of Easter? Is it just another season, another marketing gimmick? The newspaper reports that Easter is second only to the Christmas season for the marketing and purchasing of toys. Can you believe it? Strip away all the candy, eggs, plastic grass, bonnets, white shoes, pastel colors, lilies, bunnies, baskets, new dresses, parades, and what do you have left?

Do you ever reflect on the meaning of Easter in July or October? Do you take the time to consider what Jesus did on the cross at a time of year when you are not normally reminded of it? Do the crucifixion and resurrection pop into your mind on a day other than Good Friday, Easter, or a communion Sunday?

Why not do that today? Allow the memory of what Christ did to bring you pleasure and ecstasy. Let that reminder cause you to celebrate the forgiveness you have experienced.

————————

*Father, thank you for allowing Jesus to die for me. Remind me of
that event today.*

Delight yourself also in the LORD, and He shall give you the desires of your heart. —PS. 37:4

Franklin recalled to a friend the time his father gave him his first credit card: "Son, here is your very own platinum credit card. You can charge anything you want and there is no credit limit. It's your choice how and when you use it."

"I couldn't believe what my father said," explained Franklin. "At first, I thought of all the things that I could ever want. Clothes, books, travel, maybe borrow the money for a down payment on a house, car, boat, furniture, education, studying abroad. You name it, I dreamed it.

"But then I began to think about why my dad gave it to me. It was because he loved me, not because he felt guilty or was trying to buy my love. I found myself asking for his advice before I used it. Many times, I already knew if the decision was right or wrong or if it was a good investment, but I still wanted to know his opinion and to get his guidance. In the end, I found myself listening to his heart and his dreams for how his fortune should be used. Ultimately, I invested it in others rather than spend it on myself."

Father, help me to treasure and to carry out the desires you have placed within me.

Then I will go to the altar of God, to God my
exceeding joy, and on the harp I will praise
You, O God, my God.   —PS. 43:4

Have you seen pictures of my grandson Jackson?"
asked Jack. "He is the cutest little guy you've ever
seen. He's just starting to walk and is toddling all over
the place. Did I tell you about my sixteen-year-old
granddaughter, Denice? She sang the lead in her
school play. She's got talent, I tell you. How about
twelve-year-old Jonathan? We went to his baseball
game last week and had two doubles and a home run.
I'll bet he gets drafted by a professional team some day
if he keeps this up."

Ever been around someone who waxed eloquently
about the exploits of their kids or their grandkids?
Once they get started, there's no stopping them. You
can pull the plug and it doesn't phase them a bit.

Part of the enjoyment of a person or an event is in
talking about it and telling others. Their joy is expressed through overflowing praise.

If people listened to you, could they tell what your
pride and joy is? _____

Father, help me to bubble over with praise for who you are and what
you have done for me.

DISPLAYING JOY

*Serve the LORD with gladness; come before His
presence with singing.*
                                    —PS. 100:2

The statement has often been made, "Worship is
something that starts at 11:00 sharp and ends at 12:00
dull." That's closer to the truth than we want to admit.

Many a child, teenager, or adult has been dragged
kicking and screaming to church, resisting all the way.
They may be there physically, but where are they
mentally?

An African church leader once made the statement,
"People in America go to church because it is something to do while my people go to church because they
want to worship God."

Kind of convicting, isn't it? Why is it that our worship is so far from what Scripture says it should be?
Why does it seldom resemble what God desires it to
be?

The psalmist says that we are to approach worship
with a smile on our face and a song in our hearts. Our
spirits are to be lifted up in praise to God. Kind of hard
to do that with a frown on your lips or when your mind
is on the afternoon's football game. Rather than a di-
version, worship is to be a delight.

How do you approach worship?

Father, give me a glad heart that praises your name.

Does not rejoice in iniquity, but rejoices in truth.
—1 COR. 13:6

Boy, I knew it. I told you I was right. I knew he could not be trusted. He was scum and I'm glad he got caught. I hope they throw the book at him and the judge never lets him out of prison. He deserves to spend the rest of his life rotting in jail, and I hope he gets what he deserves. What a jerk!"

"I cannot believe it! Another leader fell because of moral indiscretion. That makes me want to sit down and cry. I had my differences with him and the position that he took on certain issues, but I never wanted to see this happen to him. We need to pray for him."

Whenever another prominent leader falls, regardless of whether he is a Christian or not, the responses of people usually fall somewhere between the two positions above. One cries, "Off with his head!" while the other simply cries. One's heart is hardened and cries for justice, while the other's is broken and prays for mercy. The one rejoices in another's misfortune while the other only feels remorse.

What's your response when a leader falls?

Father, may another's difficulty not be my source of joy.

DISPLAYING JOY

*. . . and the little hills rejoice on every side . . . they
shout for joy, they also sing.* —PS. 65:12, 13

Ask your average person what time of year he enjoys
the most and chances are his answer would be either
autumn or spring.

After a long, hot summer with sweltering heat and
humidity that makes you wish you'd taken a shower,
right after you took one, you long for fall. You can't
wait for the cool, crisp mornings, or the sound of a
football being kicked. Now, while those things are welcome aspects of the season, the thing most people look
forward to is the changing color of the trees, shifting
from green to vibrant yellows and flaming reds. Because of the dramatic change and the short life of the
color, it is a stunning season.

After a gray, dreary, lifeless winter, nothing is more
spectacular than spring. When the bright green buds
appear on barren trees, when the tulips, daffodils, and
hosta come out of hibernation—nothing is as grand
and glorious—but especially as welcome as spring.
The world has come alive again.

God has done a marvelous work in creation.

*Lord, thanks for sharing the beauty of creation with us. Help me to
enjoy it today.*

My son, if your heart is wise, my heart will
rejoice—indeed, I myself.   —PROV. 23:15

Son, use your brain for more than a hat rack. God gave you a brain. Please use it."

If he heard that once, Mark had heard that statement from his father one thousand times. The worst thing about that phrase was that he started hearing himself say it to his son. It was bad enough he was repeating a tired, tactless cliché. It was even worse that he was always critical of his son.

It wasn't that he was just being critical. He really did want his son to think through his decisions and make good choices. Nothing pleased him more than when his boy wrestled with an issue and made the right choice. That encouraged him that the boy had a bright future ahead of him. His problem was he did not know how to communicate how good it made him feel, and how proud he was when his son did right.

Father, help me to tell my kids when they do something that pleases me.

DISPLAYING JOY

I will delight myself in Your statutes; I will not forget Your word.
—PS. 119:16

Do you remember what it was like to become a father for the first time? You brought a camera into the delivery room to take pictures of the baby the minute he or she was born. You videotaped the first two years of her life; you recorded the first time he rolled over; when she first sat up. You treasured the memory of her first steps. You bronzed his baby shoes, and filled up twelve photo albums.

But that was nothing compared to her first words. You hung on every syllable, and you repeated "dada" over and over again, trying to get him to say your name. You knew this was the smartest kid in the world because she talked so clearly so soon. You and your wife recorded the date and the words in his baby book.

In the same way that we treasure and value our children's words and conversations, we are to take pleasure and experience ecstasy in the Word of God. We don't want to miss out or forget anything he communicates either.

_____

Father, help me to place a high value on reading and studying your word.

DISPLAYING JOY

The light of the eyes rejoices the heart, and a good report makes the bones healthy. —PROV. 15:30

They called him Mr. Sunshine. At the age of eighty-eight, Phil was the most popular volunteer in the hospital. It seemed like the mood in a room changed the minute he walked through the door. With his wealth of stories and self-deprecating mannerisms, he had a knack of turning patients' attention away from themselves. Feeling bad and full of self-pity before his visit, they were soon laughing and smiling broadly.

The medical field has recently discovered the healing power of laughter. One's mental attitude has a direct link with one's physical health. Some retirement centers have started using pet therapy. A friendly dog or cat can have a tremendous healing effect for someone who is ill or lonely.

Today, why not try to smile at everyone who frowns or looks detached? You'll be surprised at how it will change their mood.

Father, help me to share with others the joy you have given me.

So let each one give as he purposes in his heart, not grudgingly or of necessity; for God loves a cheerful giver.

—2 COR. 9:7

When it came time for the offering plate to be passed, Paul always felt as if someone put a knife to his ribs and whispered in his ear, "Your money or your life." Granted, the voice may not have been that threatening, but it sounded like, "If you don't put something in, your neighbors are going to think you're a miser." Reluctantly, he would grab a couple of ones, wad them up so no one could tell how much it was, and ceremoniously drop them in the plate. Heaven forbid if all he had was a twenty! He hoped that never happened.

In contrast, Pete loved to give. For him, it was the best part of the service. He got more out of the offering than he did the music or the sermon. After praying and planning about what to give, he felt that he was actually playing a vital part in what went on. The ministry had a piece of himself in it. He relished the knowledge that he was making a difference.

Father, help me to give of myself and my money with joy.

JULY 26

*But let all those rejoice who put their trust in You;
let them ever shout for joy, because You defend
them; let those also who love Your name be joyful
in You.*

—PS. 5:11

In the midst of a hurricane, earthquake, or natural disaster, the most popular people in town are those who operate the Red Cross shelters. In time of disaster, they provide help and relief. They dispense food, blankets, shelter, and a place to spend the night.

Go to a country ravaged by famine or war and you'll discover the same thing. The people who are highly revered are those from the Red Cross, a U.N. peace keeping force, or a famine relief agency. In fact, during Desert Storm and the famine in Somalia, the people of Kuwait and Somalia did not want the U.S. forces to leave because they provided protection and relief.

When we experience relief from spiritual famine and protection from oppression, how much more do we rejoice in the God who gives us refuge? When he shields and supports us, we have cause to rejoice and sing for joy.

------

*Father, help me to rest in your protection today. Help me to know
that I am safe.*

DISPLAYING JOY

> *. . . they . . . went to their tents joyful and glad of heart for all the goodness that the LORD had done . . .*
>
> —1 KINGS 8:66

The team had just returned from two weeks in Spain where they had participated in a series of evangelistic meetings and concerts. The team of twenty-five had done everything from concerts to puppet shows to literature distribution to sharing their testimonies at public meetings to being interviewed on radio to . . . You name it, they had done it!

Coming back, they told of how God had miraculously provided contacts with key government officials, how he stopped a rain storm just before a concert was to start and held off the rain until after they were done. They reported how the believers in Spain had been encouraged by their testimonies and were challenged to become bolder in their own witness.

As the people who were in church that evening went home, they rejoiced in how God had answered their prayers. They were excited and encouraged about how he had used their fellow members to encourage and build up the church in Spain. "If God could do that there," they told themselves, "think of what he could do here as well."

Father, help me to share with others what you have done for me.

DISPLAYING JOY

Let the heavens rejoice, and let the earth be glad;
and let them say among the nations, "The LORD
reigns."
—1 CHRON. 16:31

News of the king's heart attack quickly spread throughout the empire. As he lay near death, his loyal subjects sat by their phones, radios, and televisions, anxiously awaiting news of his condition. While the king's health was a concern, of course, of far greater importance was who would take over once he died. After all, he was ninety-two, and it was only a matter of time. Would the prince, his son and rightful heir, be crowned the next king, or would the power-grabbing Duke of Chester seize control for himself?

Within days, the dust had settled and the news was spread: The king died peacefully in his sleep, the duke was ousted and now in exile, and the prince sat on the throne. The headlines proclaimed joyfully, "Long live the King!"

We can rejoice that the King of the universe, having survived an attempted coup by the forces of evil, sits peacefully on his throne. Peace reigns and his subjects can rejoice.

Lord, I have great joy, knowing that you are in control of my life and the universe.

DISPLAYING JOY

I have set the LORD always before me; . . .
Therefore my heart is glad, and my glory rejoices;
my flesh will also rest in hope.   —PS. 16:8–9

Daddy, I'm scared," said six-year-old Johnny. "Can I crawl in bed with you and Mommy?"

"What's the matter?" asked his father, knowing the answer already. They were in the midst of the worst thunderstorm he could ever remember. He had even jumped a couple of times at how loud the noise was. It sounded like it was right over the top of them.

"The thunder scares me. I'm afraid it's going to come back again."

"Sure, you can lie here for a little while. We'll carry you back to your bed after the storm stops," his dad said as he rubbed his son's head.

In spite of the noise, his son fell fast asleep with a smile on his face. Being with Mom and Dad was all the security he needed.

In the same way, we can rest peacefully and with a smile on our lips, knowing that we are safe in the arms of God.

_____

Father, thanks for the security you bring in the midst of life's storms.

Therefore I take pleasure in infirmities, in reproaches, in needs, in persecutions, in distresses, for Christ's sake. For when I am weak, then I am strong.
—2 COR. 12:10

I can't believe that verse means it's better to be weak than strong. What in the world was Paul thinking about when he wrote it?" said Scott to the Bible study group. "Man, I hate just being sick, let alone being insulted, persecuted, or in difficult circumstances."

"I used to feel the same way," interrupted Bob, "until I tore up my knee last year and had to use crutches and a cane for three months during the recovery and rehabilitation. You remember what I went through during the physical therapy? The first thing I had to overcome was my own pride and self-pity. Once I did that and admitted that I needed my therapist and the crutches and the cane, well, then I was finally on the road to recovery. It wasn't until I started depending on others that my strength returned, not only physically, but I think my character got stronger as well."

God allows us to experience weakness, not to tear us down, but to teach us to depend on him.

Father, teach me to lean on you all the time.

DISPLAYING JOY

This is the day which the LORD has made; we will rejoice and be glad in it.
—Ps. 118:24

With a quick glance at the headlines or listening to the upcoming news stories at the top of the hour, it doesn't take a rocket scientist to conclude that there is not a lot of joy in the world. Riots, bombings, wars, famines, broken promises, scandals, moral bankruptcy, lack of integrity—yes; but joy, no. In fact, there's not much that should make us want to smile. No one in his right mind would walk outdoors and start rejoicing. What's there to be glad about, anyway?

If nothing else, we can at least find joy in the fact that God created today and has allowed us to be alive to enjoy it. We can be glad that God has provided salvation for us and has given us forgiveness, not only from the penalty of sin, but also from the guilt of sin. We can be pleased as we reflect on what Jesus did for us on the cross.

If that doesn't give you cause to rejoice, what will?

Lord, let me praise you today for your grace and salvation.

DISPLAYING JOY

AUGUST

Be on Your Guard

*He shall cover you with His feathers, and under His
wings you shall take refuge; His truth shall be your
shield and buckler.*

—PS. 91:4

A pastor in the Midwest was walking with a farmer
through the barnyard following a fire. All that remained was the charred timbers of the barn. Dejected
and downcast, they encountered the smoking remains
of a hen. "Even the hen is gone," he spat out. With a
gesture of remorse and anger, he gave the smoldering
hulk a swift kick. From underneath came the scurrying
and chirping of three little chicks. To her final dying
breath, that hen protected her chickens. Her faithfulness was their sure refuge. Her life became their
shield.

As fathers, we need to protect our children. Although we can never take God's place or provide the
type of security that he does, we still want our families
to feel secure. We want to ensure that our home is a
place of refuge and refreshment for guests. We want
our wives and children to know that we are faithful to
them so that they can rest securely.

*Father, grant me the grace and the strength to protect my family and
to keep them secure.*

Flee also youthful lusts; but pursue righteousness, faith, love, peace with those who call on the Lord out of a pure heart.
—2 TIM. 2:22

As national sales manager for an investment firm, John was away from home about 120 days a year. After a long day of meetings, he would retire to his hotel, read for an hour, and then go to bed. But tonight he couldn't sleep. He decided to go downstairs to the pool and sit in the Jacuzzi. He waded in the Jacuzzi and allowed the warm water to soothe his tired muscles. After twenty minutes, he got out and headed back to his room.

As he got on the elevator, he was joined by two attractive young women who began to flirt with him. He asked what floor they were on, offering to push the button for them. "Whatever floor you're on," they replied seductively. At that moment, he pictured his wife and two daughters waiting eagerly for him to return home. As he returned to reality, he turned to the women and replied, "No thanks, ladies, I have more important things to think about." John went back to his room, and prayed that God would never let him forget who was waiting for him at home.

God, remind me of my family when I am tempted to lust after others.

BE ON YOUR GUARD

> *For the love of money is a root of all kinds of evil,*
> *for which some have strayed from the faith in their*
> *greediness, and pierced themselves through with*
> *many sorrows.*
> —1 TIM. 6:10

Mark was a promising young salesman who appeared to be a rising star in the corporation's sales force. In each of the last three years, he had doubled his sales from the previous year and his income skyrocketed.

But as his career took off and soared, his personal life crashed on the runway. Once a promising seminary student, he had to go to work full-time when his wife had a baby. He was only going to take a year off. He took a sales position and began to achieve goals. It was hard work and required travel on the weekends, but as the money grew better, it allowed him to pay off debts and provide some nice things for his family.

As he pursued financial security, his vision clouded and he slowly drifted. Now, three years, two affairs, and one divorce later, he denies that he was ever a Christian to begin with. He was a poor pilot of his life—misjudging the horizon, ignoring his instruments, and turning off his radio, he crashed.

Father, help me to invest in the things that have lasting value.

Shepherd the flock of God which is among you,
serving as overseers, . . . nor as being lords over
those entrusted to you, but examples to the flock.
—1 PETER 5:2–3

The story is told of the owner of a factory who went out to lunch at a local restaurant. He decided to order the blue plate special. The only restriction was that there was absolutely no substitutions. He decided that he could live with that so he ordered it.

Later on in the meal, he asked the waitress for some extra butter. She politely said "No." He asked again, and she responded firmly in the negative. He called the manager over and appealed to him for some butter. He backed up the waitress and also denied the request. As the man became irate, the manager walked away. "Don't you know who I am?" he shouted at the waitress. "I'm the owner of the factory across the street." "Don't you know who I am?" she replied. "I'm the one who decides how much butter you can have."

Rather than seek to establish our personal kingdoms, we need to remind ourselves that we have been called to serve. Instead of pursuing advancement, we are to assist. Turning aside from the seat of power, I sit on the stool of the servant.

Father, protect me from the intoxication of power. Help me to serve.

BE ON YOUR GUARD

> *Therefore, my beloved brethren, let every man be*
> *swift to hear, slow to speak, slow to wrath; for the*
> *wrath of man does not produce the righteousness*
> *of God.*
> —JAMES 1:19–20

Alexander the Great was one of the few men in history who seemed to deserve his descriptive title. He was energetic, versatile, and intelligent. But while he could conquer the world, he could not conquer his own emotions. Several times in his life he was tragically defeated by anger. On one of these occasions, a dear friend of Alexander, a general in his army, became intoxicated and began to ridicule the emperor in front of his men. Blinded by anger and quick as lightning, Alexander snatched a spear from the hand of a soldier and hurled it at his friend. He only intended to scare the drunken general. But his aim was true and the spear took the life of his childhood friend.

Consumed with guilt, Alexander attempted to take his own life with the same spear, but he was stopped by his men. For several days he lay sick, calling for his friend and chiding himself as a murderer.

Alexander the Great conquered countless cities and vanquished nations, yet he was a victim of his own unbridled passion.

Lord, help me to post a guard on my anger and keep it under control.

No temptation has overtaken you except such as is common to man; but God is faithful, who will not allow you to be tempted beyond what you are able, but with the temptation will also make the way of escape, that you may be able to bear it.

—1 COR. 10:13

Physical pressure is similar to the pressure of temptation in some respects. Sometimes we can escape it on our own, but we all have our limits.

While atomic submarines are built strongly enough to batter through the ice at the North Pole, they also have a maximum crush depth limit beyond which they may not go safely. Some years ago, the submarine *Thresher* exceeded that depth. As the pressure increased, the seawater crushed the sub's heavy steel bulkheads as if they were made of cheap plastic. Searchers found only little pieces of the huge submarine.

Yet there are fish that live at the same depth. How can they survive? The answer is that they have equal pressure within themselves. In the same way, Christians face temptation on a daily basis. In ourselves we are doomed to be crushed by its pressure. But, in Christ, there is no temptation beyond our ability to resist.

Father, help me to rely on your power to withstand the pressure of temptation.

BE ON YOUR GUARD

He will not allow your foot to be moved; He who keeps you will not slumber. —PS. 121:3

Some of the most beautiful waterfalls in the world are found in Havasupai, in the bottom of the Grand Canyon—one-half mile straight down and five to six miles in. You descend into the Canyon on switchback trails and then through rocky riverbends and dry, dusty pathways, until finally you round a bend and enter a lush, green valley.

Some friends had taken a group of thirty high school students and adults backpacking into the Canyon one summer. On their way in, they arrived at the trail head in late afternoon. They had planned to go down the switchbacks in the afternoon, going as far as they could before nightfall, and camping on the trail that night. Camping in a dry riverbed, they decided to post a flash-flood watch. Each of the guys would take a two-hour shift. Our friend's wound up being from 2:00 to 4:00 A.M.! Was it ever hard to stay awake after driving ten hours and hiking for three hours.

As hard as it was to stay awake, our friend was reminded that God is always on guard for his children. He never dozes off.

Father, thank you for your faithful protection.

BE ON YOUR GUARD

He who guards his mouth preserves his life, but he who opens wide his lips shall have destruction.
—PROV. 13:3

Oops! I can't believe I said that. I'm so sorry. I really didn't mean to hurt your feelings." Ever have to eat your words like that? Ever say something you regretted? Ever wish you could retrieve something after you've spoken it? We all have.

The story is told of a village high in the mountains. One afternoon, a peasant made his way up the hill to the church where he confessed to the priest his sins of gossip and slander. He begged for forgiveness and asked what he could do to restore the relationship. The priest instructed him to take a feather pillow, tear out the seam and throw the feathers in the air. The peasant complied even though he thought it silly. Returning to the priest, he explained that he completed the task. The priest replied, "Now, go and pick up all the feathers." "Why, that's impossible," exclaimed the man. "Yes," replied the priest gravely. "It is impossible to retrieve a word of gossip after it has been spoken. You have no way of knowing how far it has spread."

Lord, help me to post a guard on my mouth, to keep watch over the things that I might say.

BE ON YOUR GUARD

*That good thing which was committed to you, keep
by the Holy Spirit who dwells in us.*
—2 TIM. 1:14

When one thinks of guarding something, many images often come to mind: the President, the Hope diamond, Fort Knox, an armored car, Secret Service agents, bodyguards, and alarm systems. These things need protection or protect something by getting it out of harm's way, by not allowing people, air, or other objects to touch it.

Another way to protect something is through constant use. It is protected because it is not allowed to decay from inactivity. Muscles are protected from atrophy through exercise. Airplanes face greater danger from lack of use by sitting on the runway than they do when flying through the air.

Rather than post a guard and put it on display out of reach of the public, the best way to guard one's spiritual gift is through constant exercise and use. It is protected from atrophy and rust. It maintains a sharper edge and does not become dull because it is constantly used.

Father, help me to exercise the gifts that you have entrusted to me.

BE ON YOUR GUARD

Keep your heart with all diligence, for out of it
spring the issues of life.   —PROV. 4:23

A recent medical report has linked being distrustful and quick to reach the boiling point with heart attacks. People who have high levels of hostility and anger and don't bother to hide it when dealing with other people are figuratively injecting poison into their hearts. Those at high risk tend to harbor a cynical mistrust of other people's motives. They get angry often and openly express their displeasure, rather than hold it in. They become strong candidates for heart attacks.

Exercise, diet, and medication are useful tools in controlling one's blood pressure. But so are patience, trust, and forgiveness. Seeking to resolve conflict and reduce tension in one's relationships can have as healing an effect on one's heart as reducing the salt in one's diet. Having realistic expectations of people and being patient and understanding in dealing with them can be preventative medicine in the same way that jogging or riding an exercise bike can be. We need to guard our heart emotionally and spiritually, as well as physically.

Father, help me to be aware of the things that weaken my heart and allow me to deal with them in a healthy manner.

BE ON YOUR GUARD

Thorns and snares are in the way of the perverse;
he who guards his soul will be far from them.
—PROV. 22:5

Growing up as an eight-year-old in Tucson, Arizona, Gene and his brother were playing in the backyard of their house. While climbing to the top of the fence, Gene lost his footing and sat square on a cactus. Yeouch! He had cactus needles in his hands, legs, and you can guess where else. From then on, he watched where he walked, stood, and especially sat. In fact, he walked a safe distance around anything that looked sharp and prickly.

The man who wants to be wise approaches evil in the same manner. For example, rather than succumb to the temptations of pornography, he avoids the magazine racks. He monitors what he watches on television or movies and has someone check up on him. Rather than take a chance on giving in, he shields himself from the temptation itself.

Father, help me to know my limits and to avoid getting close to them.

But each one is tempted when he is drawn away by his own desires and enticed. Then, when desire has conceived, it gives birth to sin; and sin, when it is full-grown, brings forth death. —JAMES 1:14–15

The other rabbits were incredulous as Jimmy told the story for the thirty-fifth time. "Fluffy carried a load of sticks, string, and a box into the clearing. He propped the box up with one of the sticks. One end of the box was on the ground and one end rested on the stick. Thus, there was a twelve-inch opening, just enough for a rabbit to crawl inside.

"He tied one end of the string to the stick supporting the box and then looped the string around a tree while he kept the end in his paw. He crawled inside the box and began eating the lettuce he had placed there. He swiftly jerked the string, causing the box to fall on top of him, trapping him inside," Jimmy said sadly.

Silly rabbit, you might think. But that is the picture James described in 1:14–15. It is the picture of someone who is tempted by his own evil desires already within him thus effectively constructing, baiting, and springing his own trap.

_____

Father, protect me from my own sinful nature. Help me to be honest with myself about the danger I face from within.

BE ON YOUR GUARD

> *But you, O man of God, flee these things and pursue righteousness, godliness, faith, love, patience, gentleness.*
> —1 TIM. 6:11

Adam would stand near the magazine rack that featured the girlie magazines, praying that God would grant him grace not to look at them. He would hold one on skiing or cars or baseball, but occasionally glance at the cover of the other ones. He would gradually inch his way closer until it was in his hands. He frantically prayed for strength as he fumbled with the pages. . . .

As he stood in the door of the casino, Jerry begged God to help him conquer his addiction to gambling. He continued to beg and plead as he walked toward the slot machines. "Oh, God, deliver me," he cried as he pulled the lever. . . .

Most of us go through life with chalk on our toes from standing too close to the line. How much better it would be to turn around, walk away, and sprint toward the presence of God.

Lord, help me to understand the things that I am drawn to and to run away from them. Grant me the grace to run into your presence and to pursue righteousness.

Let no one say when he is tempted, "I am tempted by God"; for God cannot be tempted by evil, nor does He Himself tempt anyone. But each one is tempted when he is drawn away by his own desires and enticed. Then, when desire has conceived, it gives birth to sin; and sin, when it is full-grown, brings forth death.
—JAMES 1:13–15

Fishing is a sport that rewards deception. You try to lure a fish with a bright shiny object or a juicy worm. But hidden inside that scrumptious tidbit or just the other side of that tantalizing lure is a deadly, sharp hook that will not only take away its freedom but destroy its life as well.

James says that deep within each one of us is enough bait to entice, hook, and destroy our lives. We all have desires for sex, food, sleep, material goods, pride, and power. While these are shiny and enticing, they hide a deadly hook. The desire for sex can entice one into R-rated movies and pornography, and eventually lead to adultery and a broken life.

Temptation to sin is like a credit card bill that says there is no minimum payment required. What they don't say is that you are building up interest and will eventually have to make a balloon payment to clear your debt. Unchecked lust yields sin and unconfessed sin brings death. It is only a matter of time.

Father, help me to see the hook that lies behind the bait and help me to resist giving in.

BE ON YOUR GUARD

*Where there is no wood, the fire goes out; and
where there is no talebearer, strife ceases. As
charcoal is to burning coals, and wood to fire,
so is a contentious man to kindle strife.*
                                    —PROV. 26:20–21

Because the fires of rumor spread so rapidly, a man must guard what he says and repeats to others. The subject matter for gossip is very combustible in its nature. Like a match carelessly discarded in a forest, one spark of slander or misinformation can spread havoc and destruction throughout a group of people in a very short time.

Dr. Albert H. Cantril, professor at Princeton University, ran a series of experiments to prove the velocity of gossip. He called six students to his office and, in strict confidence, informed them that the Duke and Duchess of Windsor were planning to attend a certain university dance. Within a week, this completely fictitious story had reached no less than two thousand students. The town officials were upset and phoned the university demanding to know why they had not been informed and various press agencies were frantically telephoning for details and trying to set up interviews.

As Dr. Cantril later observed, "That was a pleasant rumor—a slanderous one travels even faster."

Father, help me to speak the truth and not spread gossip.

BE ON YOUR GUARD

> *Come now, you who say, "Today or tomorrow we will go to such and such a city, spend a year there, buy and sell, and make a profit"; whereas you do not know what will happen tomorrow. For what is your life? It is even a vapor that appears for a little time and the vanishes away. Instead you ought to say, "If the Lord wills, we shall live and do this or that." But now you boast in your arrogance. All such boasting is evil.*
>
> **—JAMES 4:13–16**

Bert, a middle manager for a health management conglomerate, carries his Day-Timer everywhere. He uses it constantly for setting appointments, scheduling work and free time, and keeping track of his to-do list. James, a middle manager for the same company, prefers not to schedule appointments, but let things happen and see how the Lord leads.

Concerning the use of time, we generally swing from one end of the pendulum to the other. Regardless of whether one is rigidly scheduled or free and flexible, it is easy to become worldly by arranging life as though God did not exist. The tendency is to place ourselves in control of our destiny rather than depend on God.

We need to hold all of life with an open palm, including plans, dreams, and goals for the future.

Father, what do you want me to accomplish today?

BE ON YOUR GUARD

*So teach us to number our days, that we may gain
a heart of wisdom.*
—PS. 90:12

A friend observed, "I don't know if life is any busier than it used to be, but it is certainly much fuller. Trying to juggle work, family, ministry, friendships, small group Bible studies, kids' sporting activities, aging parents, continuing education, career adjustments, kids' music lessons. . . . Eventually things start dropping out of the sky and I start running around like Chicken Little crying, 'The sky is falling, the sky is falling.' If I am honest, I have discovered this about myself: the busier I get, the more I whine and complain about how hectic life is, but, the more I accomplish as well." As another friend aptly put it, "I've been bored and I've been busy, and I'd rather be busy."

Rather than try to accomplish everything, we should focus on finishing what is best. Instead of presenting our Day-Timer to God and telling him to bless our packed schedule, we need to ask for his wisdom in filling it out in the first place.

Father, grant me wisdom in scheduling my time and activities so that I may accomplish what will bring you the most glory.

*A fool's lips enter into contention, and his mouth
calls for blows. A fool's mouth is his destruction,
and his lips are the snare of his soul.*
—PROV. 18:6–7

You know what, Dale?" asked Arthur for the fifth
time. "You think you would learn your lesson and keep
your mouth shut. But do you? Noooooo! You have to
go and be a smart aleck. Not only did you lose your
biggest customer because of your big mouth, but you
lost your job as well."

For several years, Dale's friends continually warned
him that the sarcastic, smart-aleck remarks were going to get him in trouble. But Dale refused to admit
that he had a problem. Now, Arthur was about the only
friend he had left.

Dale's boss had warned him about his comments as
well. If he continued to rip the customers and his fellow
employees, even good-naturedly, he would find himself in the unemployment line. Well, a sarcastic memo
written in jest found itself into a customer's hands,
whereupon, greatly offended, he pulled his account.

And before he knew it, Dale was sitting in Arthur's
living room, unable to fathom the depths to which his
career had plummeted.

*Father, help me to pay attention to what I say in order to protect me
from myself.*

BE ON YOUR GUARD

He who is slothful in his work is a brother to him
who is a great destroyer.   —PROV. 18:9

The next time you're going to play cards on your computer, at least close the blinds on the window so no one can see what you're doing," Ted said to Don as a good-natured sort of jab. "You want to keep up the image that you're working, don't you?"

For the past three months, Don's motivation at work had shrunk until it was almost the size of an insect. Unable to concentrate on the accounting tasks on his desk, his mind constantly wandered. Occasionally, he would take a five-minute break to play a computer game. "Just to recharge my batteries," he told himself. Before he knew it, he was spending more time playing Solitaire and Taipei than he was trying to solve the intracacies of tax accounting.

Over time, his reputation for being lazy grew ever larger. After three months, the rumors started to fly and it was widely circulated that Don's days with the firm were numbered because he was about to be fired for laziness.

Father, help me to be diligent in my work so that I might please you.

BE ON YOUR GUARD

He who keeps the commandment keeps his soul,
but he who is careless of his ways will die.
—PROV. 19:16

One Saturday morning, Steve decided it was time to buy a new lawn mower. He went down to the local lawn and garden store and picked out the latest model. When the salesman tried to explain the safety features, Steve brushed him off saying, "I've been mowing lawns all my life. I won't have any problems."

He drove home and unloaded his new machine, and took a piece of twine and tied the safety brake in the "Off" position. With the boldness of a seasoned veteran, he attacked the area with the highest weeds. Some of them stuck in the blade. "Stupid weeds," he said with disgust, as he reached down to pull them out. As he yanked on the weeds, they yanked back and pulled his hand into the rotating blades, severing the tips of two fingers.

Three hours later, as he waited in the emergency room, he clutched his hand in pain and cursed his stubbornness, "What's it going to take to get your attention, you stupid idiot?"

Father, help me not to believe I have all the answers and don't need to listen to others.

*Diverse weights and diverse measures, they are
both alike, an abomination to the LORD.*
—PROV. 20:10

From Joshua's perspective, his younger brother Jason
was the fair-haired child who could do no wrong. He
was an excellent student, good athlete, and gifted
speaker—and never seemed to get in trouble. He was
allowed to date earlier than Joshua, stay out later, and
he even got his driver's license two years earlier than
his older brother had.

In contrast, Joshua had always struggled with the academic side of school. His interests were more in the
artistic areas of life and he was a gifted musician. As
a result of his academic problems and run-ins with the
school administration, his parents made him wait two
years to get his driver's license because "he had not
demonstrated maturity."

In Joshua's mind, it was obvious that his parents favored Jason. He had nothing against his brother, personally. It wasn't fair that his parents practiced a
double standard. Their standard seemed so arbitrary.
Why? It just wasn't fair.

---

*Father, help me not to frustrate my children by having standards and
expectations that I cannot explain to them. Help me to be fair and
equitable in my treatment of them.*

*It is a snare for a man to devote rashly something
as holy, and afterward to reconsider his vows.*
—PROV. 20:25

Betcha can't eat just one."

A popular potato chip company has built a slogan
and advertising campaign on that phrase. They have
a series of commercials that show several well-known
athletes who accept that bet. In the end, they wind up
having to shave their heads because they liked the
chips so much that they ate many and lost the bet.

While most people would not bet their hair on the
taste of a potato chip, the newspapers report countless
stories of people who bet their financial futures on
things that are less certain: auto loans, home mort-
gages, credit card debt, business contracts with delivery deadlines, etc. They justify these gambles with
statements like, "My raise next month will take care
of this." "I'm certain the production department can
meet this deadline and quota. I don't need to check
with them." Driven by a desire for comfort and the
"need" to have the latest and best model, we sacrifice
our future for the sake of today.

*Father, help me to examine my words before I speak them in order
to make certain that I can fulfill my commitments.*

But avoid foolish disputes, genealogies, contentions,
and strivings about the law; for they are
unprofitable and useless.
                                                    —TITUS 3:9

John sat in the easy chair in his living room, staring off into space. Overwhelmed and confused, he felt as if his arms and legs were tied to four wild horses, each racing off in opposite directions.

Sunday morning, a guest speaker challenged his adult class to consider their involvement in civic issues. The morning sermon focused on sharing the gospel with his neighbors. Sunday evening he attended a meeting to brainstorm ways to make his church more warm and caring. Monday evening he attended a meeting evaluating the recent men's retreat and discussing future men's ministries. From there, John went to a school board meeting considering a proposed change in the curriculum.

As he sat in his chair, questions swirled in his brain like the mist. "Where do I get involved? How do I invest my time wisely?" The more he thought, the more he struggled. "God," he cried, "help me to know what to do! Help me to invest my time wisely."

Lord, grant me wisdom so that I may use my time wisely in order to accomplish your plan and purpose for my life.

> *So the people served the Lord all the days of*
> *Joshua, and all the days of the elders . . . who had*
> *seen all the great works of the Lord which He had*
> *done for Israel . . . another generation arose after*
> *them who did not know the Lord nor the work*
> *which He had done for Israel.* —JUDG. 2:7, 10

In the late sixties, electricity was brought into a village in Nigeria. Each family got a single light in their hut. A real sign of progress. But since the people had nothing to read and many of them did not know how to read, the families would sit in their huts in awe of this wonderful symbol of technology.

The fascination with light bulb watching gradually began to replace the customary nighttime gatherings by the tribal fire, where the chiefs, elders, and tribal storytellers would rehearse the history and customs of the tribe. The tribe was losing its history in the light of a few electric bulbs.

Like Israel in the period of the Judges, without a tribal or family storyteller, it is possible to lose not only one's history and culture, but to lose one's knowledge and understanding of what God has done. If we are not careful to continually pass them on, we can lose our core values.

Father, help me to pass on to my children the lessons that you have taught me.

BE ON YOUR GUARD

*For which of you, intending to build a tower, does
not sit down first and count the cost, whether he
has enough to finish it—* —LUKE 14:28

Six-year-old Jonathan was given his first two-wheeled
bicycle by his grandmother. She had bought it at a garage sale and it needed some repairs. Early the next
morning, he and his dad went to the bike store to buy
training wheels and a new seat. Jonathan had his heart
set on a padded seat cover. He and his dad found a
nice one that they both liked, but it did not have a price
on it. Jonathan's dad took it to the clerk and asked if
she could tell him the price. It was a good thing he
asked because it was about five times what he wanted
to pay.

When it comes to following Jesus Christ as a disciple, we need to make sure that we count the cost, that
we do not go in with our eyes closed. In Luke 14:25–
35, Jesus taught several parables illustrating what the
price tag was in following him. It cost everything. But
while the price tag is high, the rewards are even
greater!

*Father, help me to be willing to pay the price of being a committed
follower.*

*If then you were raised with Christ, seek those
things which are above, . . . Set your mind on
things above, not on things on the earth.*

—COL. 3:1, 2

The story is told of Handley Page, a pioneer in avia-
tion, who once landed in an isolated area during his
travels. Unknown to him, a rat got aboard the plane
and on the next leg of the flight, Page heard the sicken-
ing sound of gnawing. Suspecting it was a rodent, his
heart began to pound as he visualized the serious dam-
age that could be done to the plane's fragile mecha-
nism.

Remembering that a rat cannot survive at high alti-
tudes, he pulled back on the stick. Climbing higher and
higher until he had difficulty breathing, Page listened
intently and finally breathed a sigh of relief. The gnawing had stopped. Upon arriving at his destination, he
discovered the rat lying dead behind the cockpit!

Sometimes we are plagued by sin that gnaws at our
life simply because we are living at too low a spiritual
level. We need to move up to a higher level where
things of the world cannot survive.

*Father, help me to be aware of the things that threaten to devour me
and help me to raise the level of my spiritual life so that they will be
defeated.*

BE ON YOUR GUARD

Pride goes before destruction, and a haughty spirit before a fall.
—PROV. 16:18

On a foggy night the captain on the bridge of a large naval vessel saw a light ahead on a collision course. He signaled, "Alter your course ten degrees south." The message came back swiftly, "Alter your course ten degrees north."

The captain then signaled, "I am a captain. Alter your course ten degrees south." Once again the reply came back, "I am a seaman third-class. Alter your course ten degrees north."

By this time the captain was furious. He signaled, "I am a battleship. Alter your course ten degrees south before we collide." This time the reply returned, "Alter your course ten degrees north. I am a lighthouse."

A lofty opinion of our own importance can blur our vision and give us a distorted picture of reality. Paralyzed by pride, we take the first step toward ruin and destruction. Unless we listen to the truth, we are on our way toward sadness and grief.

Lord, help me to take an honest look at myself rather than be puffed up with pride.

BE ON YOUR GUARD

AUGUST 28

*"And all things, whatever you ask in prayer,
believing, you will receive."*
—MATT. 21:22

A tavern was being built in a town that previously
had not allowed liquor to be sold. A group of Christians
in a nearby church opposed this and began an all-night
prayer meeting, asking God to intervene.

Lightning struck the building, and it burned to the
ground. The owner brought a lawsuit against the
church, claiming they were responsible. The Christians hired a lawyer, claiming they were innocent of
the charges. At the beginning of the trial, the judge
said, "No matter how this case comes out, one thing
is clear—the tavern owner believes in prayer and the
Christians do not."

It is easy to become hypocritical in not acting in accordance with what we claim to value. We must guard
against that lack of integrity. We need to very careful
to ensure that our behavior reflects our beliefs.

Lord, help me to be consistent in the way I live and act.

Beloved, I beg you as sojourners and pilgrims, abstain from fleshly lusts which war against the soul.
                                                    —1 PETER 2:11

Mark desperately wanted a drink of water. He had landed in Moscow, part of a group that was going to meet with educators. Because his colleagues were coming from all over the world, and because of a mix-up in flight plans, he had arrived early. As part of their preparation, they were instructed not to drink the water. The main body of the group would be bringing bottled water and water purifiers, but they were not to drink the tap water.

Not speaking any Russian, and not having any rubles, he could not order a soft drink from the cafe. "All I want is a drink of water," he cried to himself. "Why can't I just take a drink from the water fountain? What's wrong with just one drink? I'm not going to die, am I?"

Reminding himself of the possibility of sickness, he withstood the urge and waited three more hours until the rest of his party arrived. He did not want to take the chance of having one drink that could cause him to be sick, and thus miss out on a fruitful ministry.

Father, help me not to give in to the desires that pull at me and threaten to disqualify me.

BE ON YOUR GUARD

"No one can serve two masters; . . ."
—MATT. 6:24

At the outbreak of the Civil War, a Tennessee cotton-planter could not decide which side to support, the North or the South. Having friends and relatives on both sides, he decided to remain absolutely neutral. He wore a gray jacket and blue trousers, thus dressing for both the Confederacy and the Union.

Caught in the middle of a skirmish between the two armies one day, he stood up and shouted that he was neutral. He thought that they would allow him to leave the field of battle unharmed. But Union sharpshooters, seeing the gray jacket, riddled it with bullets while Confederate marksmen, seeing the blue pants, filled them with lead.

In the spiritual warfare between the forces of heaven and earth, we cannot delude ourselves into believing that we can maintain alliances with both sides. Any attempt at neutrality will leave us caught in the crossfire. We must make a choice.

God, protect me from making the wrong choice as to who I will serve with my life.

And He said to them, "Take heed and beware of covetousness, for one's life does not consist in the abundance of the things he possesses."
—LUKE 12:15

Many years ago, a major American company was having a difficult time keeping its employees satisfied working at its assembly plant in Panama. While the culture the laborers lived in was primarily an agrarian, barter economy, the company paid in cash. Since the average employee received more cash after a week's work than he had ever seen, and more than his neighbors had, he would periodically quit working, satisfied with what he had made. The typical pattern was to work for a few weeks, quit and take a few weeks off, and then come back to work and start over again.

After puzzling over the situation, company officials decided to give all their employees a Sears catalog. After that no one quit, because they all wanted the previously undreamed of things they saw in that book.

Lord, protect me from being driven by the desire to accumulate more and more.

SEPTEMBER

Stand Firm in the Faith

> LORD, *who may abide in your tabernacle? . . . He*
> *who walks uprightly, and works righteousness, and*
> *speaks the truth in his heart.*   —PS. 15:1, 2

Just north of Los Angeles, there is an amusement park that has a high observation tower. Visitors to the park can ride an elevator to the top and enjoy a magnificent view of the entire park and surrounding area. What many visitors don't know is that the tower was designed to have a sway factor of seven feet in either direction at its highest point. That means that in the event of an earthquake or high winds, the tower has the potential to sway back and forth a total of fourteen feet: The tower definitely will be shaken, but the foundation will remain secure.

David says that the true follower of God has that kind of fundamental stability. Those whose lifestyle is marked by integrity, righteous deeds, and truth can go through hard times knowing that their foundation will remain secure. They won't be shaken from their high position of godliness. They will always be welcome in God's presence.

Father, help me to sink my roots deep into you so that I may withstand the pressures and storms of life.

. . . He who does these things shall never be moved.
—PS. 15:5

An architectural wonder of stability is the Great Wall of China. Designed to protect ancient China from the barbaric hordes to the north, it was too high to climb over, too thick to break down, and too long to go around. Yet during the first hundred years of the wall's existence, China was invaded three times. Was the wall a failure? Not really—for not once did the barbaric hordes climb over the wall, break it down, or go around it. Instead, they simply bribed the gatekeepers. The Chinese placed too much reliance on a wall and not enough on the character of the gatekeeper.

Who are you when no one is looking? How high would you rate your IQ—your Integrity Quotient? On a scale of one to ten, how would you rate your truthfulness? Your personal ethics? Keeping your word? What do you need to do in order to move it up toward a "10"?

Lord, strengthen my resolve to be a man of integrity.

> *But without faith it is impossible to please Him, for he who comes to God must believe that He is, and that He is a rewarder of those who diligently seek Him.*
>
> —HEB. 11:6

The California coast was shrouded in fog that 4th of July morning in 1952. Twenty-six miles to the west on Catalina Island, Florence Chadwick, the first woman to swim the English Channel in both directions, began swimming toward California, determined.

The water was numbing cold that July morning, and the fog was so thick she could hardly see the boats in her own party. More than fifteen hours later, numbed with the cold, she asked to be taken out. Her mother and her trainer, in a boat alongside her, told her they were near land. They urged her not to quit. But when she looked toward the coast, all she could see was the dense fog. They pulled her out only half a mile from shore.

Hours later, when her body began to thaw, she felt the shock of failure. To a reporter she blurted out, "Look, I'm not excusing myself. But if I could have seen land, I might have made it." Fog blinded her reason, her eyes, and her heart.

It is difficult to have faith when we are in the fog. In the course of our lives, we face unknown situations and we must trust God for the outcome.

Lord, help me to trust you even when I cannot see the outcome.

*Let a man so consider us, as servants of Christ and
stewards of the mysteries of God. Moreover it is
required in stewards that one be found faithful.*

—1 COR. 4:1–2

When Jim was in college, he was asked to substitute
teach in his college Sunday school class. But he neglected to prepare and ended up playing a tape on
prayer by a well-known speaker. He did not keep the
trust given to him.

In contrast is the Roman sentinel who guarded the
city of Pompeii. When the city was destroyed by the
eruption of Mt. Vesuvius, many people were buried in
the ruins. Some were found in deep vaults, fleeing in
vain from the encroaching destruction. Others were
found hiding in lofty chambers. The Roman sentinel
was found at the city gate, his hands still grasping his
weapon. While the earth shook beneath him, while the
ashes and cinders fell on him, he stood at his post. He
was found there a thousand years later.

As a father, I'm not expected to stand still and be
buried by volcanic ash—or by active five-year-olds. But
I am expected to be trustworthy and faithful. I have
been given a trust.

Lord, may my children find me faithful.

STAND FIRM

> *Your word is a lamp to my feet and a light to my path.*
>
> —PS. 119:105

Two years ago, a major December storm dumped two feet of snow on Seattle in twelve hours. Unprepared, the city ground to a halt. Motorists were stranded as cars spun off roads and into ditches. With much of the city built on hilly terrain, many people abandoned their cars and walked because they could not drive up the icy inclines.

In one home near a major intersection, a woman had turned on her Christmas lights in the afternoon because it was so dark outside. Many motorists stopped and asked if they could use the phone to call a loved one and tell them they were OK or to phone a tow truck for help.

The Word of God is like those Christmas lights. It shines in the midst of darkness. Its brightness can lead us to a place of refuge, safety, and renewal. It attracts those who are searching and points them to the answers they seek.

God, may your Word light my path and direct my life.

*But be doers of the word, and not hearers only,
deceiving yourselves. For if anyone is a hearer of
the word and not a doer, he is like a man
observing his natural face in a mirror; for he
observes himself, goes away, and immediately
forgets what kind of man he was.*

—JAMES 1:22–24

Last year, Bob was traveling in a foreign country.
During one stop, he stayed at a camp. Rising early the
next day, he stumbled into the bathroom to shower
and shave. After rubbing the sleep from his eyes and
turning on the water, he stared blankly at the wall.
There was no mirror! "How am I going to shave?" he
thought. "Would I miss half my mustache or trim one
of my sideburns an inch higher than the other?"

James points out that far too often, we treat the
Word of God in the same manner. We read it and walk
away, without ever thinking how to apply it to our
lives. We quickly forget what it says, while patting ourselves on the back for having read it.

Instead, we must do more than merely read the
Bible. We need to ponder its implications for our lives.
"How am I to act differently? How does this passage
my marriage? In what way will I be more effec-
father if I follow these instructions?"

n my life as I listen to your Word.

FIRM

> *Then Joshua called the twelve men . . . and Joshua*
> *said to them: . . . "each one of you take up a stone*
> *on his shoulder . . . when your children ask in time*
> *to come, saying, 'What do these stones mean to you?'*
> *Then you shall answer them that the waters of the*
> *Jordan were cut off . . . And these stones shall be*
> *for a memorial to the children of Israel forever."*
> —JOSH. 4:4–7

Following the death of Moses, the children of Israel were poised on the eastern bank of the Jordan River, ready to enter the Promised Land. They awaited the orders of General Joshua, the new leader who had been appointed by God. God's initial marching order to Joshua was to erect a twelve-stone memorial as a vivid reminder of God's deliverance. They were to do this so that they would not forget.

As I write, I look around my office and I see various objects that remind me of people, places, and significant events in my life. Every few days, I record in a journal prayers that God has answered, things he has taught me in my devotions, and ways in which I see God's handiwork.

These all stand as memorial stones to remind me of God's grace and leading. Someday, I will pass them on to my children, teaching them the lessons I have learned and instructing them how to establish stones of remembrance in their lives as well.

Father, help me to never forget how you have demonstrated your love and grace in my past.

STAND FIRM

> *As you therefore have received Christ Jesus the*
> *Lord, so walk in Him, rooted and built up in Him*
> *and established in the faith, as you have been*
> *taught, abounding in it with thanksgiving.*
> —COL. 2:6–7

It was the worst storm in ten years. Stately trees, once thought invincible, were snapped like match sticks. Many were uprooted on the spot and blown over. As the experts examined the trees, their conclusion was simple—the branches of the trees went out farther than their roots went deep.

Leonard Holt was a middle-aged, hard-working lab technician who worked at the same Pennsylvania paper mill for nineteen years. A Boy Scout leader, an affectionate father, a member of the local fire brigade, and a regular church attender, he was admired as a model in his community. Then one day he stuffed two pistols into his coat, drove to work, stalked into his shop, and began shooting with calculated frenzy.

Deep down within the heart of Leonard Holt rumbled the giant of resentment because he had been passed over for promotion several times. Like a tree whose roots are cut off, his anger choked off everything that brought him life and nourishment. It was only a matter of time before he toppled over. His branches went farther than his roots went deep.

Father, cause me to sink my roots deep in you so that you might nourish them and keep them strong and growing.

STAND FIRM

"Ask, and it will be given to you; seek, and you will find; knock, and it will be opened to you. For everyone who asks receives, and he who seeks finds, and to him who knocks it will be opened."
—MATT. 7:7–8

Edmund Gravely and his wife, Janice, left Rocky Mount-Wilson Airport in North Carolina in their small plane to fly to Statesboro, Georgia. As the plane crossed the North Carolina/South Carolina border, Edmund died at the controls. Janice radioed for help: "Won't someone help me? My pilot is unconscious." But authorities were not able to reach her because she kept changing channels. Eventually, Mrs. Gravely made a rough landing, injured herself, and had to crawl for forty-five minutes to a farmhouse for help.

Far too often, we cry out to God for help but switch channels before his message comes through! We turn to other sources such as people, books, or seminars for help.

The instruction of Jesus in Matthew 7:7 is not to simply ask, seek, or knock one time. It is to ask and keep on asking, seek and keep on seeking, knock and keep on knocking. We are to be persistent in making our request known to God, and we must be equally determined to stay on the same channel so we can hear his answer.

Father, help me to be diligent in prayer, both in asking as well as in listening for an answer.

STAND FIRM

And when John had heard in prison about the works of Christ, he sent off two of his disciples and said to Him, "Are You the Coming One, or do we look for another?"
                                                    —MATT. 11:2–3

Blair couldn't believe his eyes. The monitor listing airline departures said his flight to New York had been canceled. He was supposed to fly to Kennedy airport and meet a group heading for Russia.

He waited patiently in line for two hours waiting to be reticketed. By the time his turn came, he had missed all the connecting flights to New York. He would have to take a completely different flight on a different airline and fly all the way to Moscow by himself. Frustrated, perplexed, and unnerved, he thought of Romans 8:28 and mentally shouted at God. "God! I love you and I believe that I have been called and that I'm serving your purpose. But how can this be good? How are you going to turn this into good?"

Like John the Baptist, you can trust God's plan even when you cannot trace it. John had certain expectations of Jesus and when he wound up in prison, he began to have doubts. Jesus' reminder was to base his conclusions on the evidence. Since he was performing the actions that had been foretold of the Messiah, John could rest assured that Jesus was indeed the Messiah.

Lord, thank you that you are in control of the details of my life. Help me to have confidence in your plan.

STAND FIRM

And you will seek Me and find Me, when you search for Me with all your heart. —JER. 29:13

One summer day in 1795, a young boy by the name of Daniel McGinnis was exploring Oak Island, off the coast of Nova Scotia. In the midst of a clearing in the woods, Daniel believed he found the site of buried treasure. Returning the next day with shovels and two friends, the boys began digging. They found a shaft thirteen feet wide, filled with clay and loose, sandy soil. Ten feet down they struck a platform of oak logs. They found another at twenty feet—and still another at thirty.

Daniel returned several years later as an adult to resume the search. He encountered additional platforms at regular intervals. At ninety-eight feet, a worker's crowbar struck a large object that felt like wood—a treasure chest perhaps? Convinced that success was near, the men went home to rest until daylight returned. The next morning, they found the pit filled with sea water.

The treasure remains hidden. For two centuries, it has both frustrated and fascinated treasure hunters. It is as if the treasure has said, "The harder you search, the less you will find. I will prevent you from uncovering my riches." What a contrast that is to the one God has given us. *You will seek Me and find Me when you seek Me with all your heart.*

Father, help me to seek for you like I would a hidden treasure.

STAND FIRM

Wait on the LORD; be of good courage, and He shall strengthen your heart; wait, I say, on the LORD!
—PS. 27:14

Sometimes it seems as if God has led us down a long hallway and ushered us into a room with a huge sign over it that says, "WAITING ROOM." It is a place where life is put on hold and it seems as if progress has come to a screeching halt. It seems as if we spend most of our time waiting; waiting for a loved one who is ill, waiting for a change in a job situation, for our family conflict to go away, for our kids to grow up and get out of school. In our frustration and anguish, we cry out, "How long, O Lord? When are you going to do something?"

Our greatest fear in waiting for the Lord is that we will discover that we've wasted our time. Fortunately, in Psalm 25:3, David declares, ". . let no one who waits on You be ashamed." In this psalm, David is asking God to teach him his ways and to lead him in truth. He confesses his dependence on God, and he asks God to protect, guide, and pardon him. As he reflects on his request, he declares confidently that the time he has spent with God has been worth whatever he sacrificed to do it. He knows that God will not allow him to be ashamed.

Lord, help me to wait patiently for your answers.

STAND FIRM

*I wait for the LORD, my soul waits, and in His word
I do hope. My soul waits for the LORD more than
those who watch for morning—I say, more than
those who watch for the morning.*

—PS. 130:5–6

John was recounting his latest adventure at camping. "Why is it that whenever I go camping, I can't sleep? I looked at my watch: 2:30 A.M. I rolled over and tried to get comfortable . . . maybe if I prayed for awhile: 2:45 A.M. Maybe if I tried counting sheep . . . : 3:00 A.M. I was exhausted, uncomfortable, cold, miserable, and on top of that, I had a headache from too little sleep. Well, I thought to myself, the sun will be up in a couple of hours, at least then I can get warm. In the meantime, maybe if I think through tomorrow's activities . . ."

In the same way that a sleepless person waits for the morning, when we wait on the Lord, we anticipate what he will do in our lives. We have a heightened sense of expectation of how he will answer our prayers or how he will demonstrate his power and control. We envision what he will do and how our lives will be different. Waiting for the Lord involves more than simply the passage of time. It also means to anticipate or to expect something to happen.

Father, help me to believe that you will do great things in my life.

But I am like a green olive tree in the house of God; I trust in the mercy of God forever and ever. I will praise You forever, because You have done it; and in the presence of Your saints I will wait on Your name, for it is good.
—PS. 52:8–9

What does it mean to wait on God's name? Rather than naming a child after a relative or famous person, a person's name in Scripture often indicates his character. Then it makes sense—we can wait on God's name because it tells us who he is. Jehovah, "the self-existent one who reveals himself"; El Shaddai, "Almighty God"; El Elyon, "God most high"; Jehovah-jireh, "The Lord will provide."

Knowing that God's name is El Shaddai, "The Almighty God," lets us know that no problem is too hard for God. Knowing that God is Jehovah-jireh, "The Lord will provide," can help us to understand that God will provide for our needs. Knowing that God is kind can help us cope with the illness or death of a loved one. Knowing that God is just can help us to endure a job situation where we are discriminated against.

We can wait on the Lord because his various names reveal his character. It lets us know that God is who he says he is and that he can be trusted.

Father, thanks for the security of trusting in you.

STAND FIRM

Then God appeared to Jacob again, when he came from Padan Aram, and blessed him. . . . So Jacob set up a pillar in the place where He talked with him, a pillar of stone; and he poured a drink offering on it, and he poured oil on it. And Jacob called the name of the place where God spoke with him, Bethel.

—GEN. 35:9, 14–15

Jacob was a man who rode a spiritual roller coaster for most of his life. He started out at a low point when his character was revealed as deceptive. From there he climbed to the top of Bethel where he vowed to serve God. He plunged headlong into a battle of deception with his uncle Laban. Recovering, he climbed back up to Peniel and wrestled with God. But he plunged into strife as his sons dealt with rape and murder. He pulled out of his freefall and returned to Bethel, rededicating his life to serve God.

Jacob's mountaintop experiences were filed under "exciting spiritual experiences of the past." Like cresting the hill of a roller coaster and plunging to the bottom, his past experience had no relation to his present life. But rather than be filed away in the halls of memory, God wanted to be Jacob's daily resource rather than his occasional recourse.

Father, help me to walk with you and grow in a more consistent manner.

STAND FIRM

Then Jacob was left alone; and a Man wrestled with him until the breaking of day. Now when He saw that He did not prevail against him, He touched the socket of his hip; and the socket of Jacob's hip was out of joint as He wrestled with him.

—GEN. 32:24–25

It was five-year-old Jonathan's first time to snow ski. Getting off the rope tow, he turned and faced the challenge of the bunny slope. His father, keeping him between his legs, slowly and carefully snowplowed to the bottom. After that trip, he turned, expressed his independence, and said, "I can do it on my own this time. I don't need your help." Knowing that he could not get hurt on this slope, the father let him go. He went about twenty feet, with his skis getting farther and farther apart. When he reached his limit, he crashed and burned. As he lay in a heap crying, his father said gently, "Now, let me teach you."

Jacob was an independent, self-made man. He knew what his gifts and abilities were, and he relied on his own resources. Whenever God offered his help, he accepted briefly, then brushed his hand aside. Like a lifeguard who strikes a drowning swimmer in order to save his life, God had to wound Jacob in order to help him. He needed to learn to depend on God all the time. Now every time he limped, he was reminded that he needed to lean on God.

Lord, remind me to rely on your strength today.

STAND FIRM

Now, therefore, you are no longer strangers and foreigners, but fellow citizens with the saints and members of the household of God, having been built on the foundation of the apostles and prophets, Jesus Christ Himself being the chief cornerstone.

—EPH. 2:19–20

During the time he was in seminary, Doug worked for an architectural drafting firm where he detailed the structural steel for high-rise buildings. There was one thing that was constant about every building they drew. Regardless of whether the building was one story or 104 stories high, you first had to ensure that the base was adequate and strong enough to support the structure that would be built on top of it. If the foundation was flimsy, the facility was certain to be a flop.

When we become Christians and join God's household, we do not build a free-standing garage on the back of the property, but rather we are added into the walls of the house itself. The foundation, which includes the work of the apostles and prophets, was poured centuries ago without any settling or shifting. The very cornerstone is Jesus Christ himself. As a result, the structure itself is stable, strong and secure, which allows more and more people to be added as the centuries go by.

Lord, thanks for the security that I experience with Jesus as my foundation.

This hope we have as an anchor of the soul, both sure and steadfast. . . .

—HEB. 6:19

He had six hours to get his sailboat ready. The forecast was ominous and frightening—a hurricane was coming! How in the world could he prepare for gale force winds and crashing breakers? Should he get every rope he had and try to tie the vessel to the dock? No, that would never work. The ship would be battered against the pylons. Should he simply let it drift and hope to find it after the storm passed through? No, it would probably be driven into the cliffs outside the harbor.

As he frantically asked advice from everyone he knew, he decided to follow the wisdom of a seasoned old salt, a veteran of the sea. "Throw out four anchors in each direction from the boat," he counseled. "Anchor deep and ride out the storm."

Rather than floating down river on an inner tube, the Christian life is often a wild, white-knuckle ride through hurricane force winds. To withstand this E-ticket ride, we need an anchor that holds, that allows our vessel to survive the onslaught and not be smashed into match sticks.

Lord, help me to anchor deeply into Jesus when my faith is threatened to be blown apart.

STAND FIRM

Blessed is the man who walks not in the counsel of the ungodly, nor stands in the path of sinners, nor sits in the seat of the scornful; but his delight is in the law of the LORD, and in His law he meditates day and night. He shall be like a tree planted by the rivers of water, that brings forth its fruit in its season, whose leaf also shall not wither; and whatever he does shall prosper. —PS. 1:1–3

A recent storm blew down several trees. Walking by them, even an ignorant, untrained person could see why they fell down. They had withered from the inside out. The wind applied the right amount of pressure and presto—firewood. Somehow, their roots had ceased providing the nutrients necessary for their sustained growth.

The writer of Psalm 1 says that the secret of sustained growth and fruitfulness is to sink your roots deep into God's Word. The one who does this has a passion for Scripture. He studies it intently and ponders its meaning. He applies its truth to his life.

This passion for God's Word serves to refresh and renew his spirit. And because his roots go deep, he is able to reach farther and accomplish more.

Father, help me to sink my roots deep into your Word.

I waited patiently for the LORD; and He inclined to me, and heard my cry. He also brought me up out of a horrible pit, out of the miry clay, and set my feet upon a rock, and established my steps.

—PS. 40:1–2

Camping on the upper peninsula between Green Bay and Lake Michigan, Jack and Janice were walking barefoot in the shallow water. They were having a great time enjoying each other's company—laughing, talking, and splashing. As they admired the sunset, they suddenly turned around and noticed their three-year-old son was missing. They looked down and saw his head break the surface of the water, spluttering for air. Jack reached down, grabbed him by the shoulders, and stood him upright safely on the shore. Evidently he had lost his footing, slipped, and couldn't stand up again.

David used that same word picture in Psalm 40 to describe God's grace in his life. He felt he was stuck in quicksand. He had lost his footing and he was going down. Desperate with panic, he cried out to God. In his grace, God turned, reached down, lifted him out of the mud, and set him securely on the shore. He went on to say that God changed his attitude from panic to praise, from terror to trust.

Lord, thanks for demonstrating your grace in my life. Help me to praise you today.

STAND FIRM

Therefore, brethren, stand fast and hold the traditions which you were taught, whether by word or our epistle.
—2 THESS. 2:15

The 4 x 100-meter relay team had an excellent chance of winning the gold medal and possibly setting a new record ... if they could just hang on to the baton. It was almost a joke now, but every day in practice at least one member would miss the hand-off or pass it clumsily to the next runner.

There was an air of tension as they stretched and warmed up for the finals of the event. The gun sounded and off went the lead runner. As he rounded the turn and came to the first pass, he had a one-meter lead. The second runner took the hand-off and stretched the lead to three meters. Number three took the pass and pressed even farther ahead. Finally, the anchor man took a successful hand-off and headed for the finish line. As he broke the tape, he was greeted by his victorious teammates. They won and established a new record!

As believers, we are to successfully pass on the baton of faith to the next generation. Our task is to hold on to it tightly and then hand it off to our children and those whom we disciple, and then shout encouragement as they run on ahead with it as well.

Father, allow me to pass the baton successfully to my children and help me to train and encourage them to be faithful in carrying it to the next generation.

STAND FIRM

"... *If you will not believe, surely you shall not be established.*"

—ISA. 7:9

John and Sarah once appeared to be madly in love. While John was in seminary, he also felt responsible to provide for his family. When Sarah became pregnant, he increased to forty hours. With the increased demands at work, he started skipping his devotional time. His boss gave him more responsibility, a raise, and a promotion. The new position required that he travel and he began to be away from home more and more. With the travel came increased temptations—traveling with coworkers, social drinking, padding expense reports ... Three years later, after an affair, a battle with alcoholism, and denial that he was ever really a Christian, he stood in the midst of the courtroom and listened to the judge's verdict ...

While not everyone who neglects their quiet time will end up in a divorce court, there is a direct link between our walk with God and the rest of our life. If the foundation of our life is weakened, our entire existence is in danger of toppling.

Lord, help me to inspect the cracks in my foundation, and to work at shoring up the weak areas.

O Lord, I have heard your speech and was afraid.
—HAB. 3:2

A woman entered an ice cream parlor to buy an ice cream cone for a mid-afternoon snack. As she waited in line, who should walk up behind her but a famous movie star that she had admired for ages. Flustered, she completely forgot what she was doing. She paid her money and walked out—without her ice cream. Standing outside the store, she racked her brain to figure out what she did with it. She finally decided to face her embarrassment and go back inside. The cone was not in the metal receptacle. Where was it? Confused, she was about to exit when the movie star with cones in hand said, "Miss, if you are looking for your ice cream, you put in in your purse."

We are easily impressed with famous people. Yet, while we lose our breath and our ability to reason in the presence of our idols, we treat God with a yawn and a ho-hum attitude. When we read of the power of the sovereign Creator of the universe, we smile and say, "That's nice." The accounts of miracles done in the Old or New Testament don't even rate the same importance as the headlines in supermarket tabloids.

Father, bring my values back in line with yours. Help me to see life and people through your eyes.

Stand fast therefore in the liberty by which Christ has made us free, and do not be entangled again with a yoke of bondage.
　　　　　　　　　　　　　　　　—GAL. 5:1

An acquaintance of mine recently practiced downward mobility. He sold his home and moved into an apartment. Chasing the American dream was taking a toll on his life and family. He had the trappings of success, but he was falling deeper in debt each month trying to maintain an image of success. The luster was wearing off and it was taking too much effort trying to keep it polished. As he put it, "I was holding on too tight and it was killing me."

When we think of the freedom we have in Christ, we usually compartmentalize it, limiting it to salvation. We are free from having to work our way to heaven, from having to earn forgiveness. But God has also freed us from having to perform for the praise of others, from having to maintain an image of success. He alone is our judge and the opinions of others ultimately do not matter. He has freed us from the rat race of materialism by promising us lasting treasure in heaven for faithful service.

Why trade freedom for a slavery that doesn't buy satisfaction? I can't think of a good reason, can you?

Lord, help me not to compromise my freedom for opinions, promotions, houses, cars, raises, and perks that do not last. Help me to invest in eternity.

STAND FIRM

"Do not think that I came to destroy the Law or the Prophets. I did not come to destroy but to fulfill."
—MATT. 5:17

What do you mean, the repair will cost $395? We only paid $300 for the unit to begin with. How could the repair cost more than the unit itself?" The VCR, which *Consumer Reports* had rated very highly, was not working. And what really upset Tony was that it stopped working two weeks after the warranty ran out.

He took it in to the repair shop. The original estimate was $50 to replace one relay. After replacing it, the unit still did not work. It would require a resistor mechanism. Another $100. It still did not work. It must be the tape drive unit. Six weeks and four replacement parts later, the repair bill was totaling more than the unit cost initially.

Furious, Tony refused to pay for the repairs. In fact, he called the manufacturer to voice his displeasure. They listened calmly and offered to replace the unit for free or upgrade it to the next model for a nominal charge.

Thankfully, we serve a God whose character guarantees the completion of every project he begins, whether it is the law or his work in our lives.

Father, thank you that you can be trusted. Increase my faith to trust you more.

Commit your way to the LORD, trust also in Him,
and He shall bring it to pass.
—PS. 37:5

Do what?" they exclaimed. "Turn the boat which direction? Are you out of your mind?"

Sam and his buddies were white water rafting and rapidly approaching the Devil's Eyeball when their guide, Jeff, told them to turn the raft sideways. "This guy is trying to kill himself and take us with him," Sam thought to himself. He was ready to jump out of the boat and head for shore. But it was too late for that.

As Jeff maneuvered the raft sideways into the rapids, the friends hung on for dear life. As he scanned the river, Sam noticed a huge boulder was right in the middle of the Devil's Eyeball. At the last second, Jeff gunned the engine and the raft scooted out of the middle of the river. The current righted the boat, spun it around the rock, and carried it safely down the river.

As Sam and his party learned later, the boulder had mysteriously appeared a week ago. Evidently a change in the current had caused it to surface. A raft heading straight down river had run into it, killing three people and injuring two others. If they had not been committed to obeying Jeff's commands, he and his friends might have been next.

Lord, help me to obey your commands even when I don't understand them or cannot see the outcome.

STAND FIRM

"For My thoughts are not your thoughts, nor are your ways My ways," says the Lord. "For as the heavens are higher than the earth, so are My ways higher than your ways, and My thoughts than your thoughts.
—ISA. 55:8–9

With fifteen seconds left in the game and the Mustangs ahead by two points, the fans in the stands began to erupt deliriously. Victory was theirs. But delirium turned to dismay and disbelief when their quarterback handed the ball off to the running back, who promptly turned and ran seventy yards in the wrong direction, and fell in his own end zone. The perplexed referees called a safety to tie the game as the gun sounded the end of the competition.

While the fans screamed, the opposing coaches were the only two men who understood the consequences of the play just run. To really win the game, the Mustangs needed to outscore their opponent by seven points, not just two. Otherwise, because of their record and schedule, their opponent would win the division and advance to the playoffs even though the Mustangs took the game.

With the tie came overtime and the chance to win by the necessary margin. Taking over, they marched steadily down the field and into the playoffs as they scored a touchdown and converted the extra point. Within the span of a few short minutes, the coach had gone from goat to hero.

Father, help me to run the plays that you have diagrammed for me.

STAND FIRM

SEPTEMBER 28

*Not a word failed of any good thing which the
LORD had spoken to the house of Israel. All came to
pass.*
                                            —JOSH. 21:45

During a political campaign, many promises are
made by candidates seeking office. Some promises are
made that they hoped to keep, but did not have all the
facts and later were forced to rescind. And then there
are promises that the candidates had no intention of
keeping, but made anyway. There are usually only a
few promises that are actually kept.

Thank goodness that the promises of God are sure,
steadfast, and eternal. We can rest secure because they
are backed by the character of God himself. If he did
not fulfill them, we would have ample opportunity to
doubt whether he would fulfill the others.

How familiar are you with God's promises? Do you
know which ones he has fulfilled and which ones are
still future? Why not begin a study in the gospels and
look specifically at the promises that Jesus made? Why
not start a prayer journal where you can list your concerns and God's answers? Studying and keeping a record of God's faithfulness will encourage you to trust
him more in the future. Don't delay, start today.

*Father, help me to discover how you have kept your word in the past
and use that knowledge to cause me to trust you more in the future.*

STAND FIRM

If any of you lacks wisdom, let him ask of God,
who gives to all liberally and without reproach,
and it will be given to him. But let him ask in faith,
with no doubting, for he who doubts is like
a wave of the sea driven and tossed by the wind.
—JAMES 1:5–6

What am I going to do?" Jeff asked himself for the thirtieth time. A laid-off aerospace engineer, he felt like he was in a sailboat without a rudder. For a while, he just drifted with the unemployment tide. But now that he had received two job offers in different parts of the country, he felt like he was out at sea with the wind blowing and the waves rising. He had no idea which direction to head the boat and even if he did, he had no way to steer it.

One of the job offers would allow his family to be within one hundred miles of his wife's folks. They currently lived near his parents, both of whom were in their seventies, and in failing health. The other job had a better salary and would be near a university that his son was considering attending. One day he wanted to take one offer, the next day he wanted to accept the other one, and the day after that he wanted neither and was completely confused.

"Aarrgh! I'm so confused! What am I going to do?" Jeff asked himself for the thirty-first time.

Lord, thank you that when I am confused, I can come to you knowing that you will grant me wisdom and lead me to where you want me to be.

STAND FIRM

But be doers of the word, and not hearers only,
deceiving yourselves.
—JAMES 1:22

In college, there are only two ways to register for classes. You can either take the course for credit or you can audit the course. Taking the course for credit means attending all the sessions, taking notes, doing the term papers, projects, collateral reading, and taking the exams. If you audit the course, all you do is show up and listen to the lectures. Since you won't receive credit, you aren't required to do the work. You don't even have to take notes if you don't want to.

James explains that the Christian life cannot be audited. It must be taken for credit. When studying the Word of God, it is not enough to merely take notes and listen to the lectures. The truth of Scripture must be applied to one's daily life. Revelation demands response. As D. L. Moody once stated, "The Scriptures were not given for our information only, but for our transformation."

Father, help me to apply your word to my life. Help me to be different as a result of the time I spend reading and studying the Bible.

OCTOBER

Be Men of Courage

Then Jesus spoke to them again, saying, "I am the light of the world. He who follows Me shall not walk in the darkness, but have the light of life."
—JOHN 8:12

During a recent storm, the power in Tim's house went out shortly after putting his children to bed. Being preschoolers, they were naturally afraid of the dark and wanted Mommy and Daddy since their night lights were out. After calming their fears, he allowed them to each have a flashlight in their bed. They could turn it on any time they were afraid and it would lead them to where they would be safe. Feeling secure once again, they were able to go to sleep.

Even though we live in the midst of a darkened world, we can feel safe and secure because the light of the world, Jesus, is always with us. This light can comfort us when we are filled with terror or guide our steps when we stumble in the darkness. It can illumine our problems when we are confused and wondering which way to turn. The light of the world leads us to the safety of our heavenly Father's arms.

Father, thank you for the security that I feel because the light of the world is in me.

"For I, the LORD your God, will hold your right hand, saying to you, 'Fear not, I will help you.'"
—ISA. 41:13

On an excursion to buy a gallon of milk, John and his two-year-old daughter, Jenny, walked hand in hand through the store. Walking down one aisle, John stopped to examine something on the shelf. Without realizing it, his grip relaxed and Jenny took off. In his concentration, he didn't know she had raced around the corner and into another section.

A minute or two later, his reverie was interrupted by a high-pierced scream and a sob that could only come from his daughter. Frantically searching for her, he discovered her two aisles over, standing in the middle and sobbing her eyes out. He reached down, picked her up, dried her tears, and helped to calm her shattered nerves.

In the midst of our worries, concerns, and frightened tears, our heavenly Father reaches out, grabs our hands, and tells us not to be afraid.

Father, help me to hang on to you. Calm my worries and concerns.

He who dwells in the secret place of the Most High shall abide under the shadow of the Almighty. I will say of the LORD, "He is my refuge and my fortress; my God, in Him I will trust."
                                                    —PS. 91:1–2

Many years ago, Frederick Nolan was fleeing from his enemies during the North African persecution. Hounded by his pursuers over hill and valley with no place to hide, he fell exhausted into a wayside cave where he fully expected to be found. Awaiting his death, he saw a spider weaving a web. Within minutes, the little bug had woven a beautiful web across the mouth of the cave. The pursuers arrived and wondered if Nolan was hiding in there; but they thought it impossible for him to have entered the cave without dismantling the web. And so they went on. Having escaped, Nolan emerged from his hiding place and proclaimed, "Where God is, a spider's web is like a wall. Where God is not, a wall is like a spider's web."

God is our wall of defense. He is the one who delivers us from those who want to hurt us. He is the one who gives us the comfort and strength we need to be courageous and to endure the trials and trouble that enter our lives. _____

Lord, help me to put my trust in you today.

*Shadrach, Meshach, and Abed-Nego answered and
said to the king, ". . . God . . . is able to deliver us
from the burning fiery furnace, and . . . from your
hand . . . But if not, . . . we do not serve your
gods."*

—DAN. 3:16–18

During the second century lived one of the most in-
spiring examples of courage in the history of the
church. His name was Polycarp, and he was burned at
the stake for his faith. As an aged man, he was arrested
by the Roman authorities and brought to the arena for
execution. He was placed in front of the cheering
crowd where the Roman proconsul pressed him hard
and said, "Swear, and I will release you. Revile Christ."

Polycarp replied, "Eighty and six years have I
served him, and he never did me wrong; and how can
I now blaspheme my King that has saved me?"

The acid test of courage is the willingness not to give
in even when you stand to lose everything. Courage
means having the confidence that God can deliver
you, but even if he doesn't, you won't compromise.

———————

Father, help me to be willing to stand firm in the face of disaster.

Looking unto Jesus, the author and finisher of our faith, who for the joy that was set before Him endured the cross, despising the shame, and has sat down at the right hand of the throne of God.
—HEB. 12:2

During the 1976 Summer Olympics, Shun Fujimoto competed in the team gymnastics competition for Japan. The competition for the gold medal was fierce. In his quest for the gold, Fujimoto suffered a broken right knee in the floor exercise. Most people would have quit and gone home in agony for having come so close. But his injury did not stop him. During the next week, he competed in his strongest event, the rings. His routine was excellent and his critics raved about his performance. But he amazed everyone when he squarely dismounted with a triple somersault twist with his broken right knee. People asked him, "Why did you do it? Didn't you feel the pain?" "Yes," he replied. "The pain shot through me like a knife. It brought tears to my eyes. But now I have a gold medal and the pain is gone."

When we keep our eyes on the prize, and on the One who will award it to us, we can endure the pain and agony as we faithfully go through our normal routine.

Father, help me to focus on you and not on my circumstances.

> *"Be strong and of good courage, do not fear nor be afraid of them; for the LORD your God, He is the One who goes with you. He will not leave you nor forsake you."*
>
> —DEUT. 31:6

In an interview with Barbara Walters, General H. Norman Schwarzkopf said, "It doesn't take a hero to order men into battle. It takes a hero to be one of those men who goes into battle."

Much has been written today describing the fact that men are missing in action from the battles of life. They have decided that they are tired of being shot at, so they withdraw from the battle. They have gone A.W.O.L. or taken a dishonorable discharge. After dodging sniper fire at the office, who wants to keep watch for SCUD missiles when you walk in the door of the house? It's a lot easier to get some R & R in front of the TV than to serve as a peacekeeping force in the living room. As a result, our wives and kids are pinned down by the enemy, desperately praying that the rescue choppers will appear any minute.

Dads, we need to get back into the battle. We need to reenlist for another tour of duty. God promises to be with us. With him on our side, we can be courageous. C'mon guys, it's hero time.

Lord, help me to trust you in the midst of the battle.

BE MEN OF COURAGE

"You are the salt of the earth; but if the salt loses its flavor, how shall it be seasoned? It is then good for nothing but to be thrown out and trampled underfoot by men."
—MATT. 5:13

Salt is a unique commodity which does many things well. It can add flavor to food, act as a preservative to arrest decay, and cause one to be thirsty. Bert was a man who possessed various qualities and did many different things well.

Concerned about the effects of pornography, he decided to prevent its spread in his neighborhood. He asked the owner of the local video store to kindly remove some offending titles from the shelves. When the owner declined, he organized a neighborhood picket of the store and even checked out the videos and delivered them to the State Attorney to determine if the situation warranted prosecution.

The most amazing aspect of the whole incident was that Bert actually made friends with the owner in the process. Through his winsome way of presenting his case, he won the man over to his cause.

Father, help me to be an agent of change who arrests decay in the world around me, but one that is winsome and attractive so as not to alienate others by being self-righteous.

"You are the light of the world. A city that is set on a hill cannot be hidden. Nor do they light a lamp and put it under a basket, but on a lampstand, and it gives light to all who are in the house."

—MATT. 5:14–15

Rising through the mist and shining in the darkness is the Space Needle, the theme attraction of the 1962 Seattle World's Fair. Its architecture dominates the landscape. It can be seen for miles around. It is a landmark that can be seen from the air, the ground, or the sea. In the darkness, the flashing beacon on top of its needle penetrates the gloom and warns oncoming airplanes of its presence. It acts as a magnet that draws travelers to its majestic beauty and invites people to discover the attractions that lay around it.

In the same way, Christians are to penetrate the surrounding culture with the good news of the gospel. Rather than blend in to the background and appear similar, we are to stand out and shine our light. We can warn oncoming travelers of the ravages of sin and the hazards of their present course. We can act as a spotlight that draws the weary to a place of refuge and refreshment.

Father, help me not to be afraid to stand out in the darkness and to shine forth my light for your glory.

OCTOBER 9

Let your light so shine before men, that they may see your good works and glorify your Father in heaven.
—MATT. 5:16

Pregnant and alone at seventeen, Sandy didn't know where to turn. Her parents kicked her out of the house, and her boyfriend refused to admit he was the father. She was at wit's end. Yet it was there at the end of her hope that she met Jeff and Sandra.

While retired, Jeff and Sandra were actively involved in helping people who had a need. For some years now, they had taken in unwed mothers who needed a place to stay until the birth of their baby. They also helped other people in need.

Living near a world-renowned medical clinic, they started hosting international guests who were airlifted to the clinic for treatment. If the treatment could be done on an outpatient basis or if they needed a place to stay before or after surgery, Jeff and Sandra would take them in.

With everyone who came to stay, the questions were the same. "Why are you doing this? What is different about you? Why are you so giving when I can never hope to repay your kindness?" Their answer would be the same to all. "It's the grace of God."

Father, may I live in such a way that your name is praised as a result of my actions.

> *"Blessed are those who are persecuted for righteousness' sake, for theirs is the kingdom of heaven. Blessed are you when they revile and persecute you, and say all kinds of evil against you falsely for My sake."*
>
> —MATT. 5:10–11

Bob Vernon, former Assistant Chief of Police for the Los Angeles Police Department, had the crowd riveted to their chairs as he recounted the tales of how he made his first arrest as a rookie cop, and how he participated in a simulated hostage rescue as part of the training for the 1984 Olympic Games in Los Angeles. As a cop, he put his life on the line from the very first moment he pinned on the badge.

While you or I might not face life-threatening decisions, we can be thankful for the example of a man who demonstrated moral courage in the face of persistent verbal fire. If and when the time comes for us to do the same, we can be reminded that we are not alone. In addition, we can remember that the final chapter is not yet written. There is a reward waiting for those who remain faithful in the midst of persecution.

Father, may I demonstrate moral courage when others challenge and criticize what I believe in.

BE MEN OF COURAGE

*No one can serve two masters; for either he will
hate the one and love the other, or else he will be
loyal to the one and despise the other. You cannot
serve God and mammon.*

—MATT. 6:24

John, you cannot keep this up," Sam said to him.
"Don't you see what you're doing to yourself, not to
mention what's happening to your wife and kids?"

Wanting to please his wife, John had begun working
overtime in order to pay for her three-thousand-
square-foot dream house. But what began as a one-
month arrangement soon escalated into a permanent
arrangement. Three years, two new cars, one baby, a
bigger home, and a dream vacation later, John was
consistently working eighty hours a week trying to
climb the corporate ladder and to stay out of debt.

The wife he once loved never saw him and his children continually asked, "When's Daddy coming
home?" The sleekness of his sports car was wasted because the only thing he used it for was commuting to
the office.

"John, you're more committed to your job than to
your family. If you keep going in this direction, you
won't have any family left to go home to. When are
you going to have the courage to say, 'Enough is
enough'?" Sam persistently asked.

*Father, help me to honestly evaluate the commitments in my life and
to rearrange them if they are out of line with what you desire.*

BE MEN OF COURAGE

> *Now it came to pass the same night that the LORD said to him, ". . . tear down the alter of Baal that your father has, . . . and build an altar to the LORD your God . . . in the proper arrangement . . ."*
> —JUDG. 6:25–26

Over the past five years, Tom's father had drifted away from God. At one point in his life, he and his family were in church every time the door was open. Sponsors of the youth group, members of the choir, treasurer of the church—their life revolved around the church. But after his kids grew up, moved away, and started families of their own, his interest and involvement in church waned. Like a lantern running low on fuel, the light of his faith began to flicker and fade.

He began substituting other intellectual writers, and even New Age books, for his usual Bible study. The pastor of the church stopped by to speak with him one day about his lack of attendance and Tom's dad told him to keep his nose out of his business. "I no longer believe that stuff anyway," he shouted as the door slammed shut. And now Tom faced the unenviable task of trying to confront and restore his dad to the faith.

Father, grant me the courage to face the difficult challenge of confronting others who are in sin.

> . . . *"We are not able to go up against the people,*
> *for they are stronger than we. . . . The land through*
> *which we have gone as spies is a land*
> *that devours its inhabitants . . . we were like*
> *grasshoppers in our own sight, and so we*
> *were in their sight."*
> —NUM. 13:31–33

I'm just not sure I'm cut out for that job," Mark whined for the fourth time that night. "Do I really have the skills and the resources to do it? What if I fail? What do I do if I find out I don't like it?"

After seven years as a fourth-grade teacher, Mark had been asked by the District Superintendent to consider testing for a position as an elementary school principal. "You have an excellent reputation with the students, parents, community, and other teachers. You'd make a great principal. I know you can do it." Reluctantly, he agreed to take the job. Now he was only two days away from starting his new assignment as the principal of a newly opened school in the district, and he was terrified.

What giants loom in front of your path? Any problems that churn in your subconscious mind? The spies in Numbers 13 needed to be reminded that the only thing bigger than their problems was their God. Would that reminder help you as well?

Lord, remind me of how you have answered my prayers and solved my problems in the past and tell me that you can do the same today.

BE MEN OF COURAGE

You shall not follow a crowd to do evil; nor shall you testify in a dispute so as to turn aside after many to pervert justice.

—EX. 23:2

It was his first time on jury duty, and John felt like he was making a huge mistake. The prosecution's case appeared so complete and convincing. He could not argue with the facts as they were presented. The defendant's case was as flimsy as a worn-out shirt and the state had seemingly poked holes in his alibi as well. But he just couldn't shake the feeling that something was lacking . . .

His fellow jurors were pressuring him for a decision. "Surely he didn't believe that nonsense about the defendant being innocent, did he? Only a fool would believe he's not guilty. The evidence is insurmountable!" He was almost ready to give in just to get them off his back, but he just couldn't shake the feeling that the defendant might be innocent . . .

In the end, they declared a hung jury because of John's refusal to give in. Two months after the trial, new evidence came to light that proved the defendant was telling the truth and that he was innocent. John was vindicated in his stubborn refusal to give in.

Father, help me to be willing to stand for my convictions even when others pressure me to give in.

Reject a divisive man after the first and second admonition.
—TITUS 3:10

Because of the emotional baggage he carried with him, Jess had a difficult time accepting responsibility for his life. Every lost job, failed relationship, rejected affection, and rebuffed attempt at closeness was met with blame for others and a refusal to believe that any of it was his fault.

Stoically silent on the outside, inside he was a seething, simmering volcano ready to erupt. One night he called Tim and began to vent about the latest failure in his life. After patiently listening and allowing him to blow off steam, Tim decided it was time to get "in his face."

"You know why no one wants anything to do with you?" Tim asked him point blank. "Because people think you're a volcano, ready to explode and they don't want to be in the path of your hot anger. You have great potential, Jess, but you have to get control of your anger. Until you start accepting responsibility for the present and stop blaming everyone else, you'll always be left alone. And you know what? I think you can do it!"

Father, help me to care enough about people and their future in order to overcome my fear of confrontation.

But Jesus said to him, "No one, having put his hand to the plow, and looking back, is fit for the kingdom of God."

—LUKE 9:62

When it comes to pursuing spiritual things, many of us lack the courage to let go of the past and press forward with diligence. We have not learned that it is important to burn our bridges so that we are not tempted to turn back.

Spanish explorer Cortez landed at Vera Cruz in 1519 to begin his conquest of Mexico with a small force of seven hundred men. Legend has it that his first order was to purposely set fire to his fleet of eleven ships. Presumably, his men on the shore watched their only means of retreat sink to the bottom of the Gulf of Mexico. There was now only one direction to move—forward into the heart of the Mexican interior to meet whatever might come their way.

In the same way, we must have the courage to purposefully destroy all avenues of retreat from being fully devoted to Christ. We must willingly choose that whatever price is required for being his follower, we will pay it.

Father, grant me the grace and the courage to be willing to follow you fully, no matter the cost.

BE MEN OF COURAGE

Examine yourselves as to whether you are in the faith. Prove yourselves. Do you not know yourselves, that Jesus Christ is in you?—unless indeed you are disqualified. —2 COR. 13:5

A young boy walked up to the pay phone in the back of the town pharmacy. After placing his call, he said, "Hello, sir, I was calling to see if you needed a lawn boy. Oh, you already have one. Well, is he adequate? Are you satisfied with his services or would you consider changing? Oh, he is! Thank you, I was just checking."

The pharmacist, who had inadvertently overhead the conversation, then said to the boy, "Sorry you didn't get the job, son."

"Oh no, sir," said the boy. "I've already got the job. I was just calling to check up on myself."

Far too often, we are afraid to discover what people really think of our performance. Rather than timidly wait for the opinions of others, we must have the courage to seek out and ask for people to evaluate our character and conduct.

Father, help me to have the courage to take a hard look at myself and to evaluate what I do.

"I know that You can do everything, and that no purpose of Yours can be withheld from You.
—JOB 42:2

In the movie *The Hiding Place,* Corrie ten Boom and her sister Betsy are prisoners, along with ten thousand other women, at the Ravensbruck concentration camp in Germany. In the midst of the beds, cold and hungry and lice-ridden, Betsy is leading a Bible class. One woman calls out derisively from her bunk, "If your God is such a good God, why does he allow this kind of suffering?" She displays her broken, mangled fingers and says, "I'm the first violinist of the symphony orchestra. Did your God will this?"

After an awkward silence, Corrie ten Boom speaks, "We can't answer that question. All we know is that our God came to this earth, and became one of us, and he suffered with us and was crucified and died. And that he did it for love."

Like Corrie ten Boom and Job long ago, part of suffering is learning to live with unanswered questions. Though we may not know the *why,* we can have confidence in the *who* behind the scene.

Father, grant me the courage to trust you even when I don't have all the answers.

The wicked flee when no one pursues,
but the righteous are bold as a lion.
—PROV. 28:1

Developing self-confidence starts with an incredibly easy, yet oftentimes difficult task of telling the truth.

Abraham Lincoln once said, "I always tell the truth . . . That way I only have to remember half as much."

Men who hide their secrets not only erode their self-confidence, they often ruin their relationships as well. They act as if they are standing on thin ice in the middle of a frozen lake. One false move, one unexpected phone call, and their secret is uncovered and they fall through the ice.

Tired of running scared and looking over your shoulder to see if anyone is following? Take an honest, but hard look at your past. If you're hiding something, then expect to be chased down by guilt and paranoia. But if you desire confidence and the strength of a lion, then develop a habit and a lifestyle of truth.

Father, help me to be honest with myself, others, and you.

*Let us therefore come boldly to the throne of grace,
that we may obtain mercy and find grace to help in
time of need.*
　　　　　　　　　　　　　　　　—HEB. 4:16

Do you remember what it was like to be summoned
to the principal's office? When you sat down in the
waiting room, your heart was in your throat and you
were afraid you were going to cry. You were ready to
confess to anything, even if you didn't do it, just to get
out of there. That probably has something to do with
why most of us are afraid to approach someone in au-
thority, whether they are a teacher, judge, politician,
pastor, or our boss. When it comes to asking for a favor, petitioning for a raise, keeping a counseling appointment, or paying a fine, we appear tongue-tied,
flustered, and ill at ease.

Hebrews 4:14–15 explains that the reason we can
approach God's throne with confidence is because we
have a friend who understands our temptations because he experienced them himself. As a result, we
can approach boldly and have the confidence that we
will receive exactly what we need.

———————

Father, help me not to be afraid to come to you when I am in need.

*And for me, that utterance may be given to me,
that I may open my mouth boldly to make known
the mystery of the gospel.* —EPH. 6:19

As he pulled up to the intersection, Bill was suddenly self-conscious of the music coming out of his car stereo. Since it was a warm, sunny day, he had his windows rolled down and his stereo turned up. But waiting at the red light was another car with its windows rolled down as well.

"If I pull up even with them," thought Bill, "they'll hear the Christian praise music that I'm listening to. Will they think I'm some kind of a freak? Will they give me a dirty look or yell obscenities at me?"

Casually reaching over and turning the volume down on his stereo, he eased up to the red light, carefully making sure that his car was slightly short of the crosswalk. "Since our windows won't be even, they won't be able to hear my music and I'll be safe."

Afraid that people might find out that you're a Christian? Rather than pray that you won't be discovered, why not pray for boldness and a clear testimony?

Lord, help me not to be afraid of what others think of my testimony.

*Now when they saw the boldness of Peter and
John, . . . they marveled. And they realized that
they had been with Jesus.*
—ACTS 4:13

The story is told of a magician in India who was approached by a mouse because he was afraid of a cat.
The magician agreed to turn the mouse into a cat.
Everything was fine until the cat ran into a dog. So the
magician willingly transformed the cat into a dog. A
few days later, the dog begged the wizard for help
because he had encountered a tiger. So his friend reluctantly agreed to change the mouse-turned-cat-turned-dog into a tiger. But the magician had enough
when the tiger returned in fear after meeting a hunter
with a gun. "I'm changing you back into a mouse," explained the magician, "because even though you have
the body of a tiger, you still have the heart of a mouse."

After encountering the risen Christ, Peter and John
were transformed from unlearned, timid fishermen
into men who spoke with boldness and challenged the
status quo.

*Father, may people whom I come in contact with recognize that I
have been with you.*

BE MEN OF COURAGE

Though an army should encamp against me, my heart shall not fear; though war should rise against me, in this I will be confident. —PS. 27:3

Read any good biographies of Christian heroes lately? The story of Corrie and Betsy ten Boom in *The Hiding Place? Through Gates of Splendor* or *The Shadow of the Almighty* about the life of Jim Elliot? Have you read the newspaper accounts of the persecution of believers in eastern Europe or China? Consider the writings of Don Richardson? How about *Foxe's Book of Martyrs*?

What would make someone defy a government edict, face down a firing squad, courageously stand in the coliseum before a pack of hungry lions, or walk into a jungle filled with head hunters? First is a message of hope and peace that transforms the lives of everyone who comes in contact with it. Second is the confidence that the Lord is our stregnth (Psalm 27:1) and that no one can harm us unless God wills it. And third, the confidence that we will see the goodness of the Lord (Psalm 27:13).

Even if they do not write our biography, if we live courageously for Jesus, we'll be standing in good company.

Father, grant me boldness to live for you, even if it brings opposition.

BE MEN OF COURAGE

> *By faith Sarah herself also received strength to*
> *conceive seed, and she bore a child when she was*
> *past the age, because she judged Him faithful who*
> *had promised.* —HEB. 11:11

Noah was told to build an ark even though he had not seen rain. . . . Moses was told to pick up a snake and it would turn back into his staff. . . . Moses and the children of Israel were led to the edge of the Red Sea with the Egyptian army hot on their tails and they were told not to be afraid. . . . Joshua was told to march around Jericho and do nothing and that the walls would fall down. . . . Jesus told his disciples that he would prepare a place for them in heaven. . . . Scripture tells us that Jesus is coming back again someday soon. . . .

Did you ever consider how outrageous those promises must have sounded at the time? If they were given to you, how would you respond?

The secret to believing a promise does not lie in the nature of the promise. Instead, it lies in the character of the one who gave the promise. Abraham and Sarah believed an outrageous, impossible promise because they knew that God was faithful.

Father, thank you that I can have confidence that you will do what
you say.

"Have I not commanded you? Be strong and of good courage; do not be afraid, nor be dismayed, for the LORD your God is with you wherever you go."

—JOSH. 1:9

One of the classic Disney animated films is *Dumbo*, the story of a circus elephant who could fly. Because of his large, oversized ears, Dumbo is the subject of ridicule and rejection. Forced to leave the elephant act and join the clowns, he is despondent and lonely. It is there that he meets Timothy, the circus mouse. It is Timothy who challenges and encourages Dumbo to attempt flight. Looking for a way to encourage and motivate his new friend, Timothy happens on the idea of giving Dumbo a "magic feather" that will enable him to soar. As long as Dumbo has the feather, he is confident in his ability.

As we face the challenges and obstacles before us, we do not need a magic feather to enable us to soar above our circumstances. We have the presence and power of Almighty God, who promises never to leave us or forsake us. We don't even need to hang on to him, for he holds us in the palm of his hand.

God, thanks for being with me and for never leaving.

". . . choose for yourselves this day whom you will serve . . . But as for me and my house, we will serve the LORD."

—JOSH. 24:15

Go with the flow. . . . Don't rock the boat. . . . Be a team player. . . . Work within the system. . . . Take it easy. . . .

Did you ever notice that many of our everyday sayings encourage one to conform with the prevailing opinion? We are told not to do anything that will either distinguish ourselves from the crowd or risk the ire or antagonism of those in charge. We are afraid of doing something that will risk the wrath of our peers.

How far we have drifted from the challenge that Joshua gave to Israel at the end of his life. In essence, he told them to go against the flow, to examine the direction that the prevailing culture was headed and then turn one-hundred-eighty degrees and go the other way. That requires a tremendous amount of fortitude and moral courage. It necessitates the confidence that only comes from God.

Father, grant me the courage to stand against the tide of my generation.

BE MEN OF COURAGE

But Daniel purposed in his heart that he would not defile himself with the portion of the king's delicacies, nor with the wine which he drank; therefore he requested of the chief of the eunuchs that he might not defile himself. —DAN. 1:8

Matt dreaded the date on the calendar. Each year on April 16, the all-male accounting firm he worked for went out to celebrate the official end of the tax season. Not that he was against celebrating. After all, the tax season was grueling and they often averaged eighty to ninety hours a week during those months. But this party was without wives and included heavy drinking. The last two years they brought in call girls.

In the past, Matt was one who celebrated the hardest, drank the most, and never remembered whose bed he woke up in. But nine months ago, he had become a Christian and he didn't feel comfortable even thinking about the party, let alone going to it. The guys had been teasing him for several weeks, reminding him of the past.

He just couldn't go this year. He wasn't sure how, but he had to talk to his boss and explain why he wouldn't be there.

Lord, give me the courage to explain my convictions and to avoid compromising situations.

BE MEN OF COURAGE

Now when Daniel knew that the writing was signed, . . . he knelt down on his knees . . . and prayed . . . as was his custom since early days.
—DAN. 6:10

For three years, Dennis had led a Bible study at his company. But then the executive council instituted a change in shift responsibilities and reassigned everyone's hours. Because of the changes, the Bible study, which had grown to forty-five, went to three groups of thirteen meeting at various hours of the day and night.

About six months later, a memo was circulated that no extracurricular meetings could be held in company meeting rooms. The studies, which by now had grown to three groups of twenty, scouted around and found neighboring restaurants where they could meet.

About a year later, the executive council asked Dennis to accept a transfer to the company's facility in Europe. When he arrived and settled in, he began to talk to his coworkers about starting up a group to study the Scriptures.

Lord, help me to practice my faith even in the face of opposition.

*Now, Lord, look on their threats, and grant to Your
servants that with all boldness they may speak
Your word.*

—ACTS 4:29

What's the matter with you, Steve?" asked his boss.
"Why can't you take the hint? We don't have any
grounds to fire you. But we can give you a lateral transfer and take away your responsibilities. You can keep
your seniority and benefits, but you'll have no chance
of advancing your career. You'll be in a dead end position with no future."

After becoming a Christian two years ago, Steve
wanted to tell everyone about the changes that had
taken place in his life. While being careful about sharing with people during company time, he was not shy
about doing it over lunch or during breaks. As a result,
several people had prayed to receive Christ because of
his testimony. His boss, an avowed atheist, had put up
with it for awhile, but was now trying to turn up the
heat to get Steve to stop.

"Whatever decision you make about my career is
up to you," explained Steve patiently. "But I can't stop
telling people about what Jesus has done for me."

*Lord, give me the boldness to tell others about you that can withstand
threats.*

I say to you, though he will not rise and give to him because he is his friend, yet because of his persistence he will rise and give him as many as he needs.

—LUKE 11:8

Walt," said Bruce, "we've been friends for a long time now and I've worked for you for ten years. I know it's company policy to only give raises once a year. You've been generous to me and I have no complaints. I have never asked for a raise in my life. But I've got to ask a big favor now. The cost of Jill's car accident and on-going rehabilitation has created more medical bills than I've seen in my life. We found out yesterday that the company will only pay 75 percent. But even the 25 percent is out of my budget. With two kids in high school and one in college, I don't know what I'm going to do. We had counted on Jill's income to pay for the kids' education.

"Man, I hate to beg, but is there any way you can help me out? Is there any way that the company can loan me the money? I just don't know what to do. I'm at my wit's end."

We can come to God with that same kind of boldness and be confident that he will act in our best interests.

Father, thanks for allowing me to enter your presence with confidence.

For as the body without the spirit is dead, so faith without works is dead also. —JAMES 2:26

Sam Johnson, a recent graduate from State Technical University with a 4.0 GPA in Marketing has several new and innovative ideas, but has never actually tried them out. Allison Ironwood, Assistant Director of Marketing for the Really Big Corporation for the past five years, has a ten-page list of both successful and failed ideas that she has tried. Which one would you hire for the new Marketing Director?

Janice Branch watches tennis tournaments on TV and reads *Tennis* magazine. Sandra Schultz played three years on the pro tennis circuit before injuring a knee and coached Powerhouse High to a state championship in tennis. Which one would you ask to coach your daughter in tennis?

In choosing the right person for the job, their experience, both the level of experience as well as the length of time, indicates whether or not they really know the subject and possess the skill. In the same way, the depth and quality of our faith is demonstrated in the way we live our lives. As Benjamin Franklin said, "Well done is better than well said."

Father, help me to consistently practice what I believe.

NOVEMBER

Be Strong

"I go the way of all the earth; be strong, therefore, and prove yourself a man." —1 KINGS 2:2

Dale felt like he could never please his father. His job was never prestigious enough, his salary never high enough, or his car ever fast enough. "Why can't you be like your brother, who earns a six-figure income and drives a BMW?" his father badgered him.

When Dale became a Christian in college, he and his father drifted apart. Their standards of success grew vastly different. His dad measured success by the cut of his clothes and the color of his car. Rather than be a workaholic like his father, he spent more and more time leading Bible studies and discipling young professional businessmen.

Dale had learned that manhood is not measured by external achievements. Instead, a true man demonstrates his strength by obeying God's Word.

Lord, help me to teach my children that the true measure of success is whether or not they obey your instructions, not how much money they make.

*"But you, be strong and do not let your hands be
weak, for your work shall be rewarded!"*
—2 CHRON. 15:7

In an attempt to get his body into shape, Jeff decided
to take up jogging. Starting out that first morning with
tremendous resolve to be the next Frank Shorter, he
managed to run fifty feet before he was out of breath
and forced to stop. The next day he made a quarter of
a block. By the end of the week, he was up to two full
blocks.

It was one year later that Jeff entered his first 5-K
run (about three miles). Not the fastest person in the
pack, he was determined just to finish. Regardless of
how long it would take him, it would be his lifetime
best time.

Nearing the finish line, he began to break into his
finishing kick. Jeff pictured himself breaking the tape
to the delight and cheers of his family. To his dismay,
the course bent to the left around a building and still
had at least a half-mile to go—but he struggled on to
the finish line.

Many times in the race of life, we are tempted to
stop running, go over to the side, sit down and watch
everyone else go by. At times like that, we desperately
need the grace of God to enable us to finish well.

God, help me to run my race with endurance and to finish well.

BE STRONG

*Now Abishai . . . lifted his spear against three
hundred men and killed them, and won a name
among these three . . . he became their captain. . . .*
—2 SAM. 23:18, 19

The Dallas Cowboys won the 1993 Super Bowl with
a defense that was ranked number one in the league.
The interesting thing was that no one on that defensive
unit was voted to the Pro Bowl. Individually, they were
not rated highly, but together, they dominated the of-
fenses of the other teams.

As men, we can gain tremendous strength from the
help, support, and encouragement of others. Like David's mighty men or a great football team, other men
can come alongside us and challenge us to greatness.

Who are you meeting regularly with? Are you part
of a supportive group of men? Who checks up on you?
Who challenges you to greatness? If you have a supportive group of people, great! If not, why not ask
some other men today if they would be interested in
meeting together to support one another.

*Father, help me not to exist in isolation and try to make it on my own.
Bring someone else alongside who can support and encourage me.*

BE STRONG

My brethren, count it all joy when you fall into various trials, knowing that the testing of your faith produces patience. But let patience have its perfect work, that you may be perfect and complete, lacking nothing.

—JAMES 1:2–4

When the Union Pacific railroad was under construction, part of the plan to connect St. Louis and California contained an elaborate trestle bridge to be built over a certain large canyon in the West. Before it was open for commercial use, the construction engineer wanted to test its strength. He loaded a train with extra cars and equipment to double its normal payload. He then had the train driven out to the middle of the bridge, where it was to remain for an entire day. One worker looked at him incredulously. "What are you trying to do, break the bridge?" "No," said the engineer. "I'm trying to prove that the bridge is unbreakable."

In the same way, temptation is not there to crush us under its weight, but rather is designed to prove our strength under pressure.

Father, grant me grace to endure the trials I face so that I may become strong and mature.

BE STRONG

My soul, wait silently for God alone, for my expectation is from Him. He only is my rock and my salvation; He is my defense; I shall not be moved.
— PS. 62:5–6

Security comes in many shapes and sizes: padlocks, life insurance, dead bolts, burglar bars, six-month checkups, tooth paste, alarm systems, peep holes, preventive medicine, antibiotics, health care plans, etc. All of us long for peace of mind and freedom from worry. The problem is that many of the things we turn to for security are insecure themselves.

For David, a man involved in many battles, a rock and a stronghold were extremely important. They were his front line of defense. He was dependent on these things for security. When he was behind the rock or inside the stronghold, he was safe from his enemies. Once he ventured outside the stronghold and in front of the rock, he was vulnerable to attack.

Just as the rock and the stronghold protected David in battle, so God is the source of our security when we face our daily battles. As long as we are depending on him for security, we are safe and we will not be shaken.

God, thanks for the sense of security and peace of mind that I enjoy when I trust and rely on you.

> *And what more shall I say? For the time would fail
> me to tell of Gideon . . . David . . . and the
> prophets: who through faith subdued kingdoms, . . .
> out of weakness were made strong, . . .*
> —HEB. 11:32–34

One of the best loved films of all time is *The Wizard of Oz*. It is the story of a young girl, Dorothy, who is stranded in a strange new world and tries to find her way back to Kansas. On her journey she meets a variety of strange, but wonderful, characters: the Tin Man, the Scarecrow, and the Cowardly Lion.

The three are best known for their glaring weaknesses. The Tin Man is strong but uncaring. The Scarecrow is willing to help but does not know how. And the Cowardly Lion puts up a fearsome facade, but is scared of his own tail. In the end, they overcome their weaknesses, help Dorothy pursue her goal, and are rewarded with symbols of what they thought they had lacked.

It would be nice if we could overcome our weaknesses simply by pinning a medal on our chests, having a university degree, or donning a red cut-out heart. But for us, the process is different. As we put our faith in God and trust him for the outcome, he gradually makes up for what we lack and he transforms us.

Father, may you take my weaknesses and use them as opportunities that cause me to depend on you.

BE STRONG

". . . and now, here I am this day, eighty-five years old. As yet I am as strong this day as I was on the day that Moses sent me —JOSH. 14:10–11

Sam's great-uncle lived on a farm in Iowa. At the age of ninety-two, he still had his driver's license, lived alone in a three story house, and still took care of his garden himself. The previous month found him in the hospital, but he insisted on going home so that he could celebrate his ninety-second birthday.

While Sam's uncle's physical strength and endurance was outstanding for his age, what was most impressive was his commitment to spiritual growth. He regularly read and studied the Bible, listened to radio preachers, faithfully prayed for family members, and attended church as often as possible.

While his physical health was not what it once was, his spiritual power grew stronger every day. Like limiting the radius of his driving, he made sure he was never far from the source of his strength. He continued to depend on the Lord and trust in him for the future.

Father, thank you for the legacy of godly relatives. Help me to leave that same type of legacy for my children and grandchildren.

BE STRONG

*Then Samson called to the LORD, saying, "O Lord
GOD, remember me, I pray! Strengthen me, I pray,
just this once, O God, that I may with one blow
take vengeance on the Philistines for my two eyes!"*
—JUDG. 16:28

Merv Griffin was in Las Vegas, emceeing an international bodybuilding exhibition. Having narrowed the competition down to the finalists, the judges were starting their deliberations. As they were waiting, Merv asked each of the contestants, "What is the purpose of muscles?" One after another answered him with a blank look or the shrug of their massive shoulders.

Samson never understood why God gave him muscles. Like some bodybuilders, Samson had the mistaken notion that muscles were there to be flexed, to wow the crowd, to be put on demonstration, and of course, to impress women. He neglected to ask God how he could use his strength to serve him better. He was more concerned about defending his title as "Mr. Palestine" rather than delivering God's people from oppression.

While you can only be young once, you can be immature your entire life! Samson never grew up and never fulfilled the promise that God had for him.

Father, help me to understand why you have given me the strengths I have and help me to use them to serve you.

BE STRONG

*He who is slow to anger is better than the mighty,
and he who rules his spirit than he who takes a
city.*
—PROV. 16:32

As a high school student, Dan was an all-league power forward in basketball. He had scholarship offers from twenty-two different major college programs. While never achieving stardom on the college level, he had proved to be a valuable sixth man. Fifteen years later as a middle-aged man, his athletic prowess was limited to city recreation leagues. Though he had lost a step or two over the years, his shooting accuracy had not diminished at all.

While his remarkable quickness had slowed, his incendiary temper had not. A hothead in high school and college, it was widely known around the league that the way to defuse his game was to get him angry.

In the midst of a close game, something would happen that would ignite his fuse. Soon he would inevitably curse a referee, elbow an opponent, or draw a technical foul and get tossed out of the game for fighting. He might lead the league in scoring, but he was ineffective in crunch time because his opponents knew how to neutralize his talents.

*Father, help me to gain mastery of my passions rather than allow
them to master me.*

> . . . *"My grace is sufficient for you, for My strength is made perfect in weakness." . . . For when I am weak, then I am strong."* —2 COR. 12:9, 10

The way up is down. To be a leader you must be a servant. If you cling tightly to life, you will lose it. To gain life you must give it away. The broad, easy path will ultimately destroy a person while the narrow, hard path ultimately leads to life. Many are called but few are chosen. Scripture is replete with seeming contradictions—paradoxes that challenge and confound the mind. Perhaps none is quite as challenging as the one that claims "I am the strongest when I am weakest."

Yet weakness becomes the platform that best displays the grace and power of God. When we have no power of our own, we are forced to cling tenaciously to God's powerful right arm. When life takes us out at the knees, we can lean on the one who comes alongside to help and support. When we cannot do it on our own strength, we can trust in the one who has proven himself to be the all-powerful God.

Lord, help me to admit my weakness and be willing to rely on your strength.

BE STRONG

Every word of God is pure; He is a shield to those who put their trust in Him. —PROV. 30:5

Neal sat at a table eating lunch with his fellow coworkers. After their usual appetizer of news, weather, sports, and cars, one person began ragging on his supervisor and the impossible demands he was making on him. "What kind of stupid jerk does he think he is?" they all asked.

Partway through the conversation, Neal began playing a mental tape inside his head. Three days ago, he and his wife and kids memorized Psalm 1. As his coworkers complained, he kept thinking about the person God blesses. Once the tape started, he could not turn it off or stop it. The second time through the recording, he got up and moved to another lunch table. He could not continue to listen to their gripes.

In Neal's case, the Word of God served as a shield to protect him from sin. It guarded his mind by not allowing him to participate in the gripe session.

Father, protect my mind from evil thoughts and complaints.

Beloved, do not believe every spirit, but test the spirits, whether they are of God; because many false prophets have gone out into the world.

—1 JOHN 4:1

It's amazing how many off-beat religious groups there are in the news these days—not to mention how many off-beat religious leaders. Some sound so close to the truth that it is difficult to know which ones to believe. And yet many people get caught up in a group and are ultimately disillusioned when the leader either commits a crime or disgraces himself in public.

How do you know which ones to believe and which ones to mistrust?

When the FBI trains their agents to recognize counterfeit money, rather than study the phony dollars, they have them handle the real money. They want them to be familiar with the color, markings, and texture. They require their agents to be so accustomed to the real thing that they immediately recognize the phony, simply because it doesn't measure up.

The best way to recognize counterfeit religion is by having an accurate understanding of the real thing.

Father, help me to be diligent in studying your word in order to know what I believe.

Blessed are the meek, for they shall inherit the earth.
—MATT. 5:5

As John commuted down the freeway, he was cut off by a bright red sports car. "You stupid idiot," he shouted. "Didn't you see me there? What are you trying to do? Kill me?"

As Jason waited to be seated for lunch, he complained loud enough for all to hear, "Hey, those guys came in after we did. How come they're being seated now? Did the hostess forget about us? I wonder what the manager thinks. Their tip just went out the window."

Rather than being a doormat, meekness is power under control. Gentleness or meekness is the opposite to self-assertiveness and self-interest. It stems from trust in God's goodness and control over the situation. The gentle person is not occupied with self at all. It is that disposition of spirit toward God in which we accept His dealings with us as good, and therefore without disputing or resisting. In the Old Testament, the meek are those wholly relying on God rather than their own strength to defend them against injustice.

Lord, help me to submit my power to your control and to accept whatever comes as being from your hand.

> *My brethren, count it all joy when you fall into*
> *various trials, knowing that the testing of your faith*
> *produces patience. But let patience have its perfect*
> *work, that you may be perfect and complete,*
> *lacking nothing.*
> —JAMES 1:2–4

The aroma of chili simmering in the crock pot is wafting through the air and the smell is driving John crazy with desire. His first instinct is to go upstairs, take off the lid, and sample a bite. What could it hurt?

But with great self-control, he resists that urge. Yes, removing the lid provides immediate gratification. But it also slows down the cooking process and robs some of the flavor. During the process of cooking, heat and flavor build up in the crock pot. When we take the lid off too early, we release that heat and flavor. Thus, the heat has to build up all over again while some of the flavor is lost forever. The process takes longer and the result is not as tasty.

In the same way, when we remove ourselves too early from a trial, our perseverance does not develop and our character is hindered from developing completely. Our growth may be stunted as a result.

Lord, grant me grace and strength to endure the trials that come my way.

BE STRONG

*. . . "Not by might nor by power, but by My Spirit,"
says the LORD of hosts.*   —ZECH. 4:6

Jason prepared for months for his journey into Russia. He lifted weights every other day, improving his strength so that he might better carry the luggage and boxes necessary for the trip. He rode an exercise bike three times a week, striving to improve his endurance and stamina for the month-long ministry. He studied and practiced the language for six months, in order to learn how to communicate with the people. Granted, there would be plenty of interpreters, but he wanted to demonstrate his desire to communicate. He read voraciously about the politics, history, and culture of the nation, striving to understand as much as possible about the people he would visit.

While he worked feverishly to strengthen himself physically and intellectually, he knew that all of his preparations were in vain if he did not strengthen himself spiritually. Ministry in a foreign country would not be accomplished by physical or mental prowess. It would be done through the power of God.

Father, help me to rely on your power and not on my own.

*But I discipline my body and bring it into
subjection, lest, when I have preached to others,
I myself should become disqualified.*

—1 COR. 9:27

In the 1980 Boston Marathon, a young unknown runner named Rosie Ruiz was initially declared the winner in the women's division of the twenty-six-mile race. But there was something that seemed amiss and an investigation followed. In the course of the search, it was discovered that this was only the second marathon in which she had run, she did not have a coach, she trained on an exercise bicycle while the other runners did 120 miles of road work per week, and she had not been seen by any of the other women runners in the race!

The investigation concluded that Rosie had probably ridden a subway for sixteen miles to get near the finish line. She was disqualified and lost the reward—not just the prize for finishing first, but the most lasting satisfaction of attaining a difficult goal.

As Paul exhorted, we need to discipline ourselves spiritually, not only to prevent being disqualified by sin, but also in order to complete the race.

Father, grant me grace to stay in proper shape spiritually.

But the fruit of the Spirit is love, joy, peace, longsuffering, kindness, goodness, faithfulness, gentleness, self-control. Against such there is no law.
—GAL. 5:22–23

One snowy morning at 5:00 A.M., a missionary candidate rang the bell at the examiner's home. Ushered into the office, he waited until 8:00 A.M. for his interview. At last, a retired missionary arrived and began the questioning.

"Can you spell 'baker'?" "B-A-K-E-R."

"Please add two plus two." "Four."

"Fine," said the examiner. "I believe you have passed. I'll tell the board tomorrow."

When the candidate looked puzzled, the examiner continued, "You demonstrated self-denial by leaving a warm bed on a snowy morning. You were prompt and on time. You were patient by waiting three hours. You showed no temper, aggravation, or indignation, but rather humility when I asked questions that a seven-year-old could answer. You have the strength of character we are looking for."

Lord, may my strength of character reflect that I have spent time with you.

. . . let us run with endurance the race that is set before us.

—HEB. 12:1

Sam eased himself into the starting blocks. After his usual pre-race ritual of stretching, limbering up, and mental preparation, he was ready. He was the favorite in this race, the 100-yard dash. He had been described as having unlimited potential, though he had never quite lived up to it.

In the past, he had been guilty of simply running the ninety-five-yard dash. With his blazing speed, he would accelerate in front of everyone, get a big lead, ease up, and cruise the last five yards. But in his last two races, he had been beaten at the tape by runners who caught up with him. Assuming the race was over, shifting into neutral prematurely and wearing the victor's crown too early, he had translated victory into defeat.

After an off-season of berating him for his lackadaisical attitude, his coach had taught him the importance of running the 110-yard dash. By mentally preparing for a longer race, no one could beat him in the last few yards. And now, he was poised for the first race of a new season, ready to fulfill the potential spoken of him for so long.

Father, help me to be faithful in completing the race you've laid out for me.

BE STRONG

Children, obey your parents in the Lord, for this is right. "Honor your father and mother," which is the first commandment with promise. —EPH. 6:1–2

Some years ago, Bobby Leach, an Englishman, startled the world by his daring feat of going over Niagara Falls in a barrel. Despite the danger of this harrowing experience, he came through it miraculously unscathed. Some time later, Leach was walking down the street and slipped on a small orange peel. Unaware of the danger and unprepared for the hazard, he fell and was rushed to the hospital with a badly fractured leg.

As Leach found out, we are often brought down by the little things that reach up and nip us in the shins rather than the big things. In the same way, the apostle Paul cautions Christians to be prepared for spiritual warfare. We, too, are more frequently brought down by a minor skirmish than by a major battle.

Do you have your armor on today?

Father, help me to stand firm in your strength and protect me from Satan's attacks.

My brethren, count it all joy when you fall into various trials, knowing that the testing of your faith produces patience.

—JAMES 1:2–3

We hear much today about the hazards of stress and how it is detrimental to our health. As a result, most of us attempt to follow the advice and sometimes go to great lengths to remove, or at least to reduce, the strain in our lives.

But as everyday experience often shows, stress and trials can actually strengthen a person. Sometimes a seed that falls into a mere handful of soil next to a boulder can grow into a large tree by sending its roots down to the earth, roots that firmly wedge it onto the rock. The mighty sequoia, the greatest of trees, grows best when forest fires periodically threaten its existence. While the fires certainly scar the tree deeply, they also assure the proper composition of the soil needed for the tree's survival.

Father, help me to welcome trials as friends, knowing that you allow them for my benefit.

Look not every man on his own things, but every man also on the things of others.
—PHIL. 2:4 (KJV)

During the 1960 Olympics, defending gold medalist Al Oerter and teammate Rink Babka were expected to take the gold and silver medals in the discus throw. Although Babka was very ill the night before the competition began, he was still leading his teammate after the first four throws. On the fifth and final throw, Oerter stepped into the circle, spun around, and threw the discus farther than any other that day. Snatching victory from defeat, he won the gold medal, while Babka took home the silver.

It was sometime later that it was discovered that Babka had noticed and pointed out a flaw in Oerter's technique during the fourth throw. Oerter made the small adjustment that was necessary, and it enabled him to win the gold. Though Babka was not the winner that year, no one could call him a loser.

It takes a strong man to sacrifice his own interests for the sake of another.

Father, remove any selfish motives from my heart so that I might strengthen others.

. . . God is faithful, who will not allow you to be tempted beyond what you are able, . . .

—1 COR. 10:13

Chances are you have passed a weigh station on one of your travels and seen the trucks lined up, waiting for their turn to pass over the scale. The large tractor-trailer trucks that travel on the highways of the nation are subjected to a load limit. This means that there is a limit as to how much weight each truck is allowed to carry. The reason for establishing these limits is that if the trucks were allowed to exceed their weight limit, the roads and bridges could eventually fall apart because a given road is designed to support vehicles up to a certain weight.

In the same way, God knows how much we can bear when he allows us to be tested. While we may overestimate or underestimate what we can handle, God knows the strength of our character. Because of that, he has assigned a definite "load limit" to each of us and never exceeds it.

Lord, thank you that you design my trials and tests with my strength in mind.

BE STRONG

But no man can tame the tongue. It is an unruly evil, full of deadly poison. —JAMES 3:8

The Greeks understood the difficulty of controlling the tongue. The ancient philosopher Zeno once said, "We have two ears and one mouth, therefore we should listen twice as much as we speak."

The story is told of a young man who asked Socrates to instruct him in the art of oratory. On being introduced, he talked so incessantly that Socrates asked for double his usual fee. "Why charge me double?" the young fellow asked incredulously. "Because," said the orator, "I must teach you two sciences: the one is how to hold your tongue, and the other is how to speak."

This knowledge of the tongue's power was not limited to the Greeks alone. King David went to the point of asking God to post a guard over his mouth to keep watch over what came out of his lips (Psalm 141:3).

All the strength we can muster is not enough to master our tongues. We need God's help.

Father, take my mouth and place it under your control.

Rest in the LORD, and wait patiently for Him.
—PS. 37:7

Bart, a well-known psychologist, counseled forty-five hours a week, wrote and published ten books in the past five years, and conducted marriage enrichment seminars on the weekend. He served as an assistant coach for his son's little league team and sat on the council of elders at his church. He hit the ground running at 4:30 every morning and fell into bed after 11:00 every night. He maintained a constant pace seven days a week.

After several years of this constant, frenzied pace, he gradually started becoming detached from his patients. His advice started to sound like it was being recycled, instead of the fresh insights he usually brought to his sessions. He had a harder time getting out of bed in the morning, and gradually exercised less and less.

After complaining about tiredness, his doctor told him he was fatigued. His physical reserves had been spent and were not being replenished. Instead of more discipline, he needed rest. If he didn't slow down soon, he would burn out and become an empty shell with nothing to offer.

God, help me to examine my physical reserves and make sure they get replenished.

But those who wait on the LORD shall renew their strength; they shall mount up with wings like eagles, they shall run and not be weary, they shall walk and not faint. —ISA. 40:31

Sandy joined a local health club in order to get his body into shape. On his first day at the club, one of the instructors sat down with him to plan his exercise regimen. "Sandy," said his trainer, "you said you want to get into general, all-around, good physical condition. Is that right? OK, what I recommend is that you start a program of exercising three days a week. We suggest you blend a combination of weight training with an aerobic exercise, either jogging, riding a bicycle, basketball, or racquetball."

"Why can't I lift weights and run every day?" interrupted Sandy. "Won't I get stronger if I do it more often?"

"Actually, you won't," replied the trainer. "You see, the muscles need a time of rest to recuperate and get stronger. If the muscles are always stretched and tired, your strength never builds up. It may surprise you, but in the development and building of muscles, rest is very important."

Father, help me to rest in you so that my strength may be renewed.

BE STRONG

Resist him, steadfast in the faith, knowing that the same sufferings are experienced by your brotherhood in the world.
—1 PETER 5:9

Nine-year-old Ted carried the cocoon of a moth into his house in order to watch the fascinating events that would take place when the moth emerged. When the moth finally started to break out of its cocoon, Ted noticed that it was struggling very hard to break free of its prison. Thinking he could help, he reached down and widened the opening of the cocoon and soon the moth was free.

"Dad," said the boy as he carried the moth to his father, "what's wrong with the moth? Its wings are all shriveled up."

After hearing the boy's explanation of what happened, his dad said, "Son, what you didn't realize is that the struggle to break free of the cocoon actually strengthens the moth's muscle system. Without that struggle, the moth's growth is hindered and its future is crippled."

Father, help me not to resist the trials you bring into my life. Remind me that they help me to grow stronger.

BE STRONG

*The God of my strength, in Him I will trust; my
shield and the horn of my salvation, my stronghold
and my refuge; my Savior . . .* —2 SAM. 22:3

One of the fears of this generation is the threat of
nuclear meltdown—the failure of the reactor at a nuclear power plant. Chernobyl may have had the first
one, but the experts claim there are many more acci-
dents waiting to happen.

When a meltdown occurs, where do you go for
safety? Are there enough lead suits for everyone to
wear? Enough protective gear for the local population
to feel secure?

Even beyond the fear of a nuclear winter, where
does one turn when life crashes in? When you feel
bombarded at work, what kind of protective gear do
you pull out of your desk drawer? When you suffer a
relational meltdown at home or in your neighborhood,
what do you do then?

Thankfully, we do have a stronghold, a sure refuge
in time of trouble, a shield who protects: God.

*Father, let me run to you whenever I am in danger. Thanks for being
there.*

*For the weapons of our warfare are not carnal but
mighty in God for pulling down strongholds.*
—2 COR. 10:4

Conventional warfare; chemical warfare; nuclear
warfare; psychological warfare: each one was created
to defeat a specific enemy or strike at a facet of the
enemy's arsenal or armor.

Their power is relatively small compared to the
weapons of spiritual warfare. The weapons God has
entrusted us with are designed not merely to attack,
but to demolish strongholds. Rather than being a fortress of stone or rock, a stronghold is a mental outpost,
an argument or pretense set against the knowledge of
God. "Sin has no consequences," "God won't really allow anyone to go to hell," "I am in control of my destiny," "There are many ways to get to heaven"– all are
examples of strongholds in conflict with biblical truth.

Like a conquering general leading a host of cap-
tives, our goal is to take captive every thought to make
it obedient to Christ.

*Lord, tear down any strongholds I may have erected in my life
against you.*

BE STRONG

*Then Jonathan, Saul's son, arose and went to David
in the woods and strengthened his hand in God.*
—1 SAM. 23:16

Tony," said Bill, "I just don't know where to turn. My
family doesn't want anything to do with me since I became a Christian. I was laid off from work because of
the recession, my car's transmission broke yesterday,
and the bank is threatening to repossess my house. I
thought becoming a Christian was a great idea, but
everything has gone downhill since then. What's going
on?"

Sitting down, Tony listened as Bill unburdened his
heart. Desperately wanting to follow God in his new-
found faith, he was struggling because his outward circumstances were crashing in on him. Occasionally
offering a comment or two, Tony tried to remind Bill
of who God was. He encouraged him not to rely on his
feelings, but to cling to the promises found in Scripture.

By the time they parted, Bill had something he could
hang on to.

*Father, help me to encourage someone today to look to you for
strength.*

BE STRONG

*He will guard the feet of His saints, but the wicked
shall be silent in darkness.*
—1 SAM. 2:9

"The best defense is a good offense." "Good pitching
always beats good hitting." "It's not over until the fat
lady sings." "When the going gets tough, the tough get
going." The world of sports is filled with clichés. Another cliché that is just as true is, "The best team
doesn't always win," or "The race doesn't always go
to the swift." Occasionally, the strongest team doesn't
win. The Bible points that out over and over:

David and Goliath. Gideon and the Midianites. Moses and Pharaoh. Joshua and Jericho. Daniel and the
lions. Shadrach, Meshach, Abed-Nego and the fiery
furnace. Esther and Haman.

Strength is not the most important asset when going into the battle. The real questions is, "Whose side
is God on?" He is the One who guards, protects, and
ultimately brings victory through his might, sometimes snatching it from the jaws of defeat.

Lord, help me to trust you to fight my battles for me.

BE STRONG

DECEMBER

Do Everything in Love

But, speaking the truth in love, may grow up in all things into Him who is the head—Christ.
—EPH. 4:15

You could hear the din all the way down the street. Jason, with the self-proclaimed gift of confrontation, was attacking his two daughters again. He gave them a verbal tongue-lashing about their room looking like a pigsty, their grades not being high enough, and their poor choice in friends. Before long, they were cowering in the corner like a couple of whipped puppies.

Every time Jason lit into his family, Donna, his wife, tried to smooth his ruffled feathers. She would laugh nervously and try to divert his attention, or at least, to change the subject. Rather than incur his wrath for expressing her opinion, she acted as if nothing happened. After he cooled down, she baked his favorite cookies and avoided mentioning his latest tantrum.

Rather than drift to one extreme or the other, Scripture tells us that we are to tell the truth in love. In addition, we are to love in truth. An extreme of truth can lead to the harsh standard of legalism which no one can measure up to. An extreme of love can produce a sweet, sticky sentimentalism that avoids conflict at all costs.

Father, as I raise my children, help me to weave together the strands of love and truth.

EVERYTHING IN LOVE

*"Be angry, and do not sin": do not let the sun go
down on your wrath.*
—EPH. 4:26

During the summer in Barrow, Alaska, the northern-most U.S. city, the sun stays up for eighty-three days. On the day it does set, it only falls from sight for twenty-seven minutes. If you take Paul's words literally, that's a long time to stay angry!

Rather than give permission for one to be angry for up to twenty-four hours a day, this phrase means that we are to keep short accounts of our conflict. In the world of finance, bank tellers reconcile and balance their accounts at the end of the day. They cannot carry over a shortage or overage to the following day. Each day they start afresh. In the same way, we are to reconcile our conflicts quickly rather than carry them with us into a new day, relationship, or event. When we are offended or when we offend others and a relationship is broken, we need to forgive and clean up the pieces.

God, help me not to hold grudges.

> *"But if the servant plainly says, 'I love my master,*
> *my wife, and my children; I will not go out free,'*
> *then his master shall bring him to the judges.*
> *He shall also bring him to the door, or to the*
> *doorpost, and his master shall pierce his ear*
> *with an awl; an he shall serve him forever."*
>
> —EX. 21:5–6

A brilliant, talented young concert pianist was giving the first concert of his professional career. As he played skillfully through his program, the audience sat in rapt attention, hardly able to take their eyes off the young musician. At the conclusion of his performance, the audience exploded into a standing ovation. All were on their feet, except for one old man at the front. But the young pianist went off the stage crestfallen and dejected.

Afterward, the stage manager came up to him full of congratulations and praise, but the young pianist said, "I was no good, it was a failure." The manager responded, "You didn't fail! It was tremendous! Look out there, everyone is on his feet except one old man!" And the young pianist responded, "Yes, but that one old man is my teacher."

As a husband, father, employee, and leader, our service is not to be motivated by the applause of the crowd. It is to be motivated by our love for the Master.

Lord, help me to tune out the applause of others and concentrate on pleasing you.

Sacrifice and offering You did not desire; my ears You have opened; burnt offering and sin offering You did not require. Then I said, "Behold, I come; in the scroll of the Book it is written of me. I delight to do Your will, O my God, and Your law is within my heart."

—PS. 40:6–8

True servants are those whose lives are characterized by a joyful attitude and conduct. They respond as David did, "I delight to do Your will, O my God." The word for desire carries the idea of eagerness, delight, or taking pleasure in something. A servant is one who does his task with joy and eagerness. There are some things we do in life because we're committed to do them. We may complain, but we'll do them because they are important. You may jog because you're committed to keeping your body in shape—you don't enjoy the sideaches, the tiredness, the pain, or the sweat. On the other hand, there are other things we do because they bring us joy. You probably look forward to playing with your children because you love to see and make them laugh. So while jogging may become drudgery and playing with your kids may be fun, you do both because you know that God wants you to care for your body and your family.

Father, help me find satisfaction in every step of obedience to you.

EVERYTHING IN LOVE

For you, brethren, have been called to liberty; only do not use liberty as an opportunity for the flesh, but through love serve one another. —GAL. 5:13

In 1863, Abraham Lincoln issued the *Emancipation Proclamation,* declaring that every man was free. Thousands of slaves gained that freedom at the end of the Civil War. With this freedom came a choice as to how they would live: as servants or as free men.

History records another declaration of freedom that presented slaves with the choice of how they would use their freedom. In Galatians 5:13, Paul says, "You, my brothers, were called to be free. But do not use your freedom to indulge the sinful nature; rather, serve one another in love" NIV.

Through his death on the cross, Jesus Christ bought us out of the slave market of sin and set us free. As free men, we now have the choice as to how we will live. Paul exhorts us to use our freedom, not to pursue our own selfish interest, but to serve one another. Albert Schweitzer echoed the call when he said, "I don't know what your destiny will be, but one thing I know; the only ones who will be really happy are those who have sought and found how to serve."

Lord, teach me what it means to be a servant.

Now the purpose of the commandment is love from a pure heart, from a good conscience, and from sincere faith.

—1 TIM. 1:5

The famous philosopher Linus Van Pelt once said, "I love mankind; it's people I can't stand." With that one concise statement, he summed up both the challenge and difficulty of life: loving people. We are to both show love to people and to produce love in their lives.

Paul's words are written in the context of a discussion about false teachers who neither showed love nor produced love. They were solely concerned with communicating knowledge. Rather than waste his time cultivating intellectual giants, Paul wanted to produce men and women who loved God.

As fathers, we must focus our efforts on cultivating a love for God in our children's hearts. This necessitates that we model and demonstrate it.

Father, help me to fall in love more deeply with Jesus and may everyone around me see that in my life.

Love does no harm to a neighbor; therefore love is the fulfillment of the law. —ROM. 13:10

This was the last straw. He had told Dave, his next-door neighbor, not to park in front of his house. But would he listen? Nooo! Well, Bill would get even this time. He turned on his sprinklers and aimed them to be sure that Dave's car was drenched. And what a co-incidence that the passenger window was down. Too bad, if only he had listened.

John ran his document through the copier. The light flashed, "Paper jam." As John looked, unsure of what to do, he cried out, "All right, who jammed the copier? Why couldn't the secretaries leave it in working order for me?"

An attitude of love demands that we take responsibility for our actions rather than blame others. It means that we seek to serve rather than to control. We protect instead of pilfer. Love does no harm to its neighbor.

_____

Father, help me to keep my neighbor's best interests at heart.

But, speaking the truth in love, may grow up in all things into Him who is the head—Christ.

—EPH. 4:15

Don had made the blunder of blunders. In bidding the construction job, he misplaced the decimal point on one of the elements of the specifications. And now that the company got the job, their profit margin had gone from adequate to razor thin with no room for overruns. And here he sat in the general partners office, trying to explain how he was going to manage the project to ensure they didn't lose money.

"Of all the stupid mistakes!" ranted George. "Why couldn't you double-check your figures? Haven't you learned anything around here? You know our procedures—double-check your work and then have someone else go over it as well." "Calm down, George," soothed Campbell. "It's not like you never made a mistake. We'll survive. It's not like he killed someone. Don't be so hard on him. We cannot afford to lose him over a silly mistake."

Lord, allow me to be more honest and caring in my communication and relationships.

*And above all things have fervent love for one
another, for "love will cover a multitude of sins."*
—1 PETER 4:8

I don't understand you, Don!" exclaimed Jim. "When
you were asked if there was anything to disqualify me
from being considered for this position, you didn't say
anything. You, above all people, are well acquainted
with my past. You know about the drinking, gambling,
and affairs. If that doesn't disqualify me, I don't know
what does. Why did you recommend me to the church
for this ministry, anyway?"

"Jim, I don't look at you and see your failures," explained Don for the seemingly hundredth time. "Those
things happened a long time ago. As far as I am concerned, you are a completely different person. The
man who did those things no longer lives. Since you
committed your life to Jesus, you have grown steadily.
Even though you may not see yourself in that light, a
great many people look up to you as an example of
spiritual maturity and leadership. You are ready to be
considered for this position of leadership."

"Thanks for reminding me again, Don," said Jim. "I
appreciate your love and encouragement. You have believed in me when I couldn't believe in myself.
Thanks."

---

*Father, help me to express my love by not reminding my wife, kids,
and friends of how many times they have failed.*

EVERYTHING IN LOVE

Hatred stirs up strife, but love covers all sins.
—PROV. 10:12

I'll forgive you, but I'll never forget what you have done!" shouted Maurice at his son, Josh. "You brought that girl into our family with her new ideas and different traditions. She's an outsider, for crying out loud! We tried to understand and accept her, hoping that you would grow out of it and break up with her. Look what you've done to our family. And now you want to marry her? Go ahead, but don't expect us to be there."

The words, shouted at Josh ten years ago, echoed in his mind as if they had been said yesterday. Now that he and Carla finally had a baby, his parents wanted to let bygones be bygones so that they could see their granddaughter. Maybe the little girl was the salve to heal their broken relationships and the cornerstone to rebuild the bridge burned long ago. But how could he mentally block out everything that was said and done?

If the flame of love for his parents had grown so cold that it could not be revived perhaps he could do it for little Jessica. Maybe his love and commitment to her future would enable him to forgive his parents for the hurt they had caused.

Father, enable me to love others enough in order to strive for reconciliation and open communication.

EVERYTHING IN LOVE

Let love be without hypocrisy. . . .
—ROM. 12:9

Hi! How'ya doing, Arthur? How's my good buddy? Doing OK, huh? Well, you have a good one." As soon as Art left, Steve muttered under his breath. "What a jerk! All he ever does is talk about how bad life is. What does he think I am, a counselor? I don't have time for this."

There are not many things people despise more than empty clichés and insincere questions. And yet like a whale blowing water, we find that we're guilty of spouting them far too often. Gulp!

If you want to be known as a man who sincerely cares for others, then you'd better have the time and be prepared to listen when you ask someone how they are doing. We need to be willing to be open and vulnerable with others in order to create a climate of trust and acceptance.

Father, help me to care deeply about the hurts of others and enable me to express it consistently.

There is no fear in love; but perfect love casts out fear, because fear involves torment. But he who fears has not been made perfect in love.

—1 JOHN 4:18

But what if he doesn't listen to me? Or worse yet, what if he gets upset and never speaks to me again? Then what will I do?" thought Jason to himself.

He had just discovered that his older brother, Mark, was involved in some questionable business investments. Now he faced the unenviable task of confronting his brother about the whole matter. While he was convinced it was the right thing to do, it would be extremely difficult and could potentially end their friendship.

In the end, Jason decided he loved his brother enough to risk his wrath and potential alienation. Better that than allow him to make a mistake and ruin his reputation.

In order to confront someone, our love for them and our commitment to them must be great enough to outweigh our fear of rejection.

Father, help me care enough to confront.

We love Him because He first loved us.
—1 JOHN 4:19

One of the characteristics of human beings is that we respond to love. Take the hardest, driest dirt, turn the soil, plant a seed, water it daily, add the right amount of nutrients, and eventually something will grow. In the same way, the hardest, most stand-offish girl, when showered by genuine love and affection through cards and gifts will eventually respond to a boy's attention.

This has huge implications for our relationships. If we want our wife and children to love us, we must initiate the process. We must listen intently and sincerely to their words and feelings. We must continue to send cards to her, telling her how much we treasure her. We must carve time out of our schedules to play with our children, taking them to the park or the zoo, without them having to beg.

Father, thank you that you loved me first, and that I did not have to perform to get your attention. Help me to demonstrate that same kind of love to those I come in contact with.

> *Brethren, if anyone among you wanders from the
> truth, and someone turns him back, let him know
> that he who turns a sinner from the error of his
> way will save a soul from death and cover a
> multitude of sins.*
> —JAMES 5:19–20

As young teenagers, Jack and his brother were invited to drive with some friends from Los Angeles to Tucson. They were to leave late Friday night and drive all night, arriving some time Saturday morning.

Jack took over driving in the wee hours of the morning. He drove through Phoenix and headed south to Tucson as the sun was coming up. About an hour later, his friends woke up and commented on the beauty of the sunrise. "Wait a minute!" they exclaimed. "Isn't the sunrise supposed to be on the other side of the car?"

In Jack's eagerness to take over driving, he misread the road signs and headed north instead of south. By the time they discovered his mistake, they were one hundred miles out of their way!

As members of the body of Christ, we are to lovingly restore brothers and sisters who have wandered away. By encouraging repentance, we help cover a multitude of sins, both those committed in the past and those they will commit in the future.

*Father, help to restore and redirect people who are wandering away
from God.*

EVERYTHING IN LOVE

Better is a dinner of herbs where love is, than a fatted calf with hatred.
—PROV. 15:17

Dinnertime was the worst time of the day for Don. His mother would slave for two or three hours preparing the meal, endeavoring to put the finest food on the table. But then Dad would come home, and everything would take on the semblance of a strafing run. Skidding his car into the driveway, he would kick whatever toys were left out and curse the kids who left them there. From there, he would gruffly slam the front door, toss his briefcase into the corner, and collapse into the rocking chair. Barking out orders for the newspaper, a cold drink, and the remote control, he intimidated his family into silence.

The only time dinner was enjoyable was when Dad was on a business trip. When he was out of town, Don's mom would usually only fix soup and sandwiches or maybe scrambled eggs and toast, but at least they could carry on a pleasant conversation without being criticized for everything under the sun.

Dad, what kind of atmosphere do you create when you come home? _____

Father, help me live in such a way that my children look forward to and anticipate my return because they enjoy being with me.

Death and life are in the power of the tongue, and those who love it will eat its fruit.

—PROV. 18:21

I really shouldn't be telling you this," the social worker sneered. "But your last case worker said that you were incorrigible." Rather than leave that meeting dejected, Steve left feeling pretty good about himself. He had misunderstood what the social worker said. "I thought she said I was encourageable," he recounted later. "So I went out and tried to encourage everybody I came in contact with. My friends got so tired of it that they were ready to kill me."

Labels, names, and nicknames can be damaging to one's self-image. But they can also provide someone with character qualities to live up to.

As parents, it may be too late to change the names of our kids. But we can do our own research about their names and explain to them what their name means or what relative they were named after. And we can encourage them to develop positive character traits as they grow and mature.

Father, help me to be wise in talking to other people. Help me to paint a hopeful future with my words and encouragement.

EVERYTHING IN LOVE

*I love the LORD, because He has heard my voice
and my supplications. Because He has inclined His
ear to me, therefore I will call upon Him as long as
I live.*
                                        —PS. 116:1–2

Having developed the art of concentrating on the newspaper or television and tuning out those around, we become a master at tunnel vision. Has your son or daughter ever called "Daddy" three or four times before you acknowledge them with a grunt? On occasion, have they snatched the newspaper out of your hands or grabbed your cheeks and forcefully turned your head until you look them in the eye?

But when we put down the paper, turn off the TV, pick them up, and put them on our lap, and look them directly in the eye, they leave saying, "I love you, Daddy. Thanks for listening."

One of the best ways to demonstrate our love for our wife and children is simply by listening to them. We can give them the gift of presence, of being fully engaged in their conversation. We communicate our love by listening and it bonds us closely together.

Father, help me to pay attention and listen to my wife and children.

> ... *"You shall love your neighbor as yourself."*
> —MATT. 22:39

Thomas Monaghan, the founder, president, and chief executive officer of Domino's Pizza, Inc., made a profound statement regarding the growth of his company. From 1970 to 1985, Domino's grew from a small, debt-ridden chain to the second largest pizza company in America with sales of over one-billion dollars.

When asked to account for the phenomenal growth of the company, Monaghan explained, "I programmed everything for growth." And what was his plan? "Every day we develop people—the key to growth is developing people."

Monaghan realized that the secret to success was not special cheese, a tasty crust, or fast delivery schedules. It was people.

Father, help me to love my neighbors by building into their lives and helping them to grow.

> *. . . God, . . . has given us the ministry of*
> *reconciliation . . . and has committed to*
> *us the word of reconciliation.* —2 COR. 5:18, 19

Elizabeth Barrett Browning's father disapproved so strongly of her marriage to Robert that he disowned her and would not speak to her. On an almost weekly basis, Elizabeth wrote love letters to her father, asking for a reconciliation. Yet never once did he reply. After ten years of letter writing, she received a huge box in the mail. Opening it, she discovered to her dismay that all of her letters were returned unopened.

Today, those love letters are among the most beautiful in English literature. If her father had only opened and read a few of them, a reconciliation might have taken place.

The Bible is God's love letter of reconciliation to a world estranged from him. Not only should we read it, but God also has given us the assignment of sharing it with the world. We are his intermediaries—his ministers of reconciliation.

Father, help me to share your message of reconciliation with someone today.

"Greater love has no one than this, than to lay down one's life for his friends."
　　　　　　　　　　　　　　　　　—JOHN 15:13

In the Billy Graham film *Shiokari Pass,* a young Christian is working for the railroad company, far away from his fiancée. He works diligently until the day comes to return to his fiancée and marry her. So he boards the final train for home.

As the train climbs a steep hill on the way home, it suddenly shakes hard and stops. Running to the front of the passenger car, he discovers that it is disconnected from the rest of the train. Slowly, it begins to roll backward down the steep slope. Having worked on the railroad, the man knows there is a sharp curve behind them that the car cannot handle. Feverishly, he tries to stop the car by using the hand brake, but it doesn't stop. Soon, the car will be thrown off, killing the passengers.

It is at this point that he remembers his favorite verse in the Bible, John 15:13 and it motivates him to do what is necessary to stop the car. While he has everything to live for, he jumps on the train tracks and stops the passenger car with his own body. He gives his life to save the lives of others.

Lord, thank you for the sacrificial love of Jesus.

EVERYTHING IN LOVE

Husbands, love your wives, just as Christ also loved the church and gave Himself for it.

—EPH. 5:25

The story is told of a prince and his family who were captured by an enemy king. When brought before the magistrate, the prisoner was asked, "What will you give me if I release you?" "Half of my wealth," was the prince's reply.

"And if I release your children?"

"Everything I possess."

"And if I release your wife?"

"Your Majesty, for her I would give myself," said the prince.

Moved by the prince's devotion to his family, the king freed them all. On the return home, the prince remarks to his wife, "Wasn't the king a handsome man?" With a look of deep love for her husband, she said to him, "I didn't notice. I could keep my eyes only on the one who was willing to give himself for my sake."

———————

Father, help me to be willing to sacrifice myself and my interests for my wife.

EVERYTHING IN LOVE

*Who comforts us in all our tribulation, that we may
be able to comfort those who are in any trouble,
with the comfort with which we ourselves are
comforted by God.*   —2 COR. 1:4

For most of his life, Paul suffered from an enlarged
heart. Oh, it was not linked to high blood pressure and
he was not susceptible to heart attacks. His heart problem came from his exposure to the grief and cares of
others. It was a heart of compassion.

As a young teenager, he got mixed up in the wrong
crowd and eventually landed in prison. His parents
and friends completely disowned him. No one wanted
anything to do with him. In the depth of his loneliness,
he came face to face with the Savior and met a friend
who would never leave.

Because of what he had gone through, he tended to
see and feel the hurts of others more easily. Many
years later, released from prison, established in his
faith, and highly respected by his church as a spiritual
leader, he was the one everyone turned to for comfort
and encouragement. People in crisis would call him in
the middle of the night. He often rearranged his schedule in order to counsel and provide a listening ear.

*Father, because you have comforted me, let me share with and com-
fort others who hurt.*

EVERYTHING IN LOVE

Though I speak . . . And though I have the gift . . .
and though I have all faith . . . and though I
give . . . but have not love, it profits me nothing.
—1 COR. 13:1–3

Mark," shouted Peter, "you are one of the most talented people I've ever met: You are an excellent teacher, you make people think beyond their standard stale answers. You have wonderful, creative ideas. You are an accomplished musician. But you know what your problem is? You're as cold as a fish. I get the impression that you don't like people. You rarely say 'hello' or smile when someone walks by. When someone begins to open up and show some emotion, it's like a wall is erected between you and them. People have the impression that all you care about is your books and your music. You communicate with your actions that you are uncomfortable with people and you can't relate to their hurts or needs. On a scale of one through ten, your ministry effectiveness is a minus four."

"People don't care how much you know until they know how much you care." This much used statement is still very true.

_____

Father, help me to express and demonstrate my concern for others.

EVERYTHING IN LOVE

Love suffers long and is kind; . . .
—1 COR. 13:4

Daddy," said four-year-old Caitlin, "will you tie my shoes?"

"Wait a minute," responded her father, "I just tied them five minutes ago. Why did you take them off?"

"My socks didn't match my shirt. I wanted to change. Please tie my shoes."

"Oh, all right, but this time leave them on."

Ever have a day when you tie the same pair of shoes thirteen times? When you cry, "Last call, the van is leaving for home," for the fifth time? When your son says, "I can't go to sleep. I'm still hungry. Can I have something to eat and a story?" for the third time in five minutes? When your daughter says, "One more kiss and hug" after you threaten to spank her for getting out of bed? When the high school principal calls and says, "I need to speak to you about your son"?

Sound exaggerated? No? More likely it's a typical day with many opportunities to show love in a patient, gentle manner.

—————————

Lord, help me to be patient and kind with my family this evening.

EVERYTHING IN LOVE

. . . love does not envy; . . .
—1 COR. 13:4

I can't believe he got a new car. And isn't he in the process of buying a new house as well? He could never afford this stuff on his salary. What did he do, rob a bank or something? It must be nice to be rich."

Now be honest. The last time a friend, neighbor, co-worker, or relative received a gift or bought something new, did one of those phrases go through your mind? Did you wish that it was you instead of him? Did you try to figure out how he could afford it, and conclude that he must have a rich uncle or had done something illegal to get the money?

How far have we come from the biblical injunction to "rejoice with those who rejoice"? Instead of taking pleasure in the accomplishments and rewards of others, we seek to tear them down and show how they really don't deserve what they have. Instead of being content with what we have, we are jealous of what they've received.

Father, allow me to be truly happy for others when they tell me of the good gifts they've received from you.

. . . love does not parade itself, is not puffed up.
—1 COR. 13:4

Do you know how many homeless people I personally ministered to last month?" asked Tom. "One hundred and fifty. Can you believe it? It was a personal record. I'll bet no one in the city gives out more food than I do. My service is going to be legendary. I'll bet God is polishing my crown right now. I'll bet my mansion in heaven is going to be humongous."

A caricature? Perhaps, though there are those who serve for the glory and the applause they receive. Quite a contrast from the saying, "There's no limit to the good that can be done if you don't care who gets the credit."

The attitude of love serves for the sake of the one in need, not the one doing the serving. It seeks to build up the fainthearted, not to bolster one's own sagging ego. Regardless of who sees or if no one sees, a truly charitable person stoops to lift up those who have fallen. He is more comfortable between the scenes than in the spotlight.

Father, help me to serve in love and to be satisfied even if you're the only one who knows.

[Love] does not behave rudely, . . .
—1 COR. 13:5

When you were dating your wife, do you remember opening the car door for her? You were offended when she got out of the car by herself before you could come around to open it. You told her that it bothered you, and you asked her to wait patiently until you could do it for her. You didn't want her to think that your parents had not taught you how to be a gentleman.

Twelve years of marriage and three children later, your attitude is, "What's the matter, is her arm broken?" Can't she see that I've got my hands full with my brief case? Why can't she open the door and get the kids in the car herself?"

Chivalry may not be dead, but based on the way most husbands treat their wives, you'd think the prognosis was terminal. Come on, guys, let's act like gentlemen and treat our wives like ladies.

Lord, help me to lovingly treat my wife with polite dignity.

[Love] does not seek its own, . . .
—1 COR. 13:5

On their tenth anniversary, Bruce took his wife out to dinner. Trouble was, he forgot to tell her that he had invited two other couples. The conversation focused on the plans the three men had to play golf on the weekend. Even though his wife had asked him to look at antiques on Saturday, he accepted the invitation of the men and even offered to get a buddy to complete the foursome.

After dinner, Bruce took a box out of his pocket and presented his wife with a ring as an anniversary gift. It was a family ring, with birthstones for each of their children. He made sure the other couples saw and commented on it before he handed it to his wife to put it on her finger.

Satisfied that everyone was pleased with his choice of jewelry, he changed the subject to his favorite pastime, tennis. While his wife tried not to look bored or hurt, he regaled the group for an hour with the exploits of the latest tournament he'd played in.

Father, help me not to use others to satisfy my need for attention.

[Love] is not provoked, . . .
—1 COR. 13:5

Paul, the head of the quality control unit, had a reputation for being picky. His perfectionistic streak caused him to rise through the corporate ranks. His careful attention to details not only saved the company millions but enhanced their fame and their competition's regard for them in the industry.

But what was his greatest asset at work turned out to be his most glaring weakness at home. His wife and children were discouraged and ready to give up because nothing they did was ever good enough to please him. It wasn't just that his expectations were unrealistically high. It was that he screamed at them when they didn't measure up to what he wanted. Rather than suggest ways to improve, he ripped their self-images to shreds.

Dads, how do your kids perceive you? Angry? Critical? Why not ask God to bring that under his control?

Father, give me the grace to control my anger so that I don't harm my family in any way.

[*Love*] *thinks no evil.*
—1 COR. 13:5

"Carol," said Ruth, "every time Jim and I have a fight, he gets historical."

"You mean he's hysterical? If you're in danger, get out of there."

"No, he's historical. He brings up every time I've failed for the past fourteen years. He refuses to forget the past and let me live down my mistakes. He keeps throwing them back in my face. And then he wonders why I don't have any confidence in myself and why I can't change. He won't let me. I think he wants me to be reminded that I'm a loser."

Gentlemen, let me encourage you to declare a moratorium on past mistakes. Do not carry grudges. Don't say, either verbally or nonverbally, "I'll forgive you, but I'll never forget it." If something has been forgiven, then agree that it is buried and cannot be used ever again as a weapon or a reminder. It cannot be used as a tool to demonstrate a pattern. Forget it.

Father, grant me the grace to choose not to remember when someone does something wrong.

[Love] bears all things, believes all things, hopes all things, endures all things.

—1 COR. 13:7

Jonathan, you're going to be the best baseball player the league has ever seen. If you keep practicing like this, you're going to be a great fielder. You'll be able to catch the ball and field grounders as well as you hit home runs."

"Amanda, you have such a pretty voice. I'll bet that people will love to hear you sing. You'll be able to use your voice to really encourage others."

Each night at bedtime, Jason tried to tell his children something different that would let them know that he believed in them. Taking an activity that he had seen them do that day, he would try to paint a bright picture of what their future might look like. He prayed earnestly that they would pick up his optimism for their development. He firmly believed that their potential was unlimited. They could be and could do anything.

Lord, help my children know that I believe in them.

Notes

1. James Patterson, *The Day America Told the Truth* (New York: Prentice Hall, 1991).

2. Kent Hughes, *Disciplines of a Godly Man* (Wheaton, IL: Crossway Books, 1991), p. 65.